"*Mashed Potatoes* . . . will add spice to your family devotions. Tim blends creative activities and life-changing truths in just the right portions to help dads in their role as a spiritual leader. I must warn you, Tim's ingenious ideas will prompt your kids to beg for more. Imagine that!"

Ken R. Canfield, Ph.D.
President, National Center for Fathering

"Hands-on, active, visual, messy, explosive and fun! . . . Biblical principles are carefully and accurately applied, with total fun and learning along for the ride."

Jim Condap, Pastor to Students

"Tim Shoemaker has done it again! . . . The activities are engaging, and the instructional guidelines clearly and thoroughly—with wonderful touches of humor—map the course for each event. I suspect that mom and dad, as well as the kids, will learn some things about the ways of God from these pages."

Robert A. Vogel, Western Seminary

"Here is an excellent and energetic tool in providing a fun way to nurture your family's faith and love for God. . . ."

Ross W. Bacon, Pastor

"Parents on the go often struggle to find meaningful points of connection with their kids. . . . Tim comes through again with a book full of how-to's that will impact your kids."

James MacDonald, Pastor

"This book could literally revolutionize the way you approach and facilitate family devotions. . . . Go ahead, jump in with both feet. You won't be disappointed! . . . The easy coaching style makes it a breeze to grasp and implement in a relatively short time the dynamic principles of God's Word. If you lead family devotions, here's your invitation to kick it up a notch with your kids."

John Zivojinovic, Pastor of Student Ministries

"If this book had been there for us when our kids were young, there would have been a lot more laughing in our household—and a lot more understanding."

Art Greco, Director of Evangelism and Prayer

"Encourages dads to step up to the plate and be the spiritual leaders in their homes."

Rob Ryg, Pastor

"Who says the Bible is dull? These devotionals will motivate and challenge your kids to mine God's Word for all it's worth."

John R. Strubhar, District Superintendent

"These devotions are creative and memorable—creative because they impact at every age level, memorable because they are fun."

Rob Bukowski, Youth Pastor

"It's refreshing to have a family devotional book that addresses relevant topics with such biblical clarity. In a world of compromise and tolerance, Tim addresses the issues head-on and brings us back to the authority of God's Word."

Colleen Ryan, Home-schooling Mother of Four

Mashed Potatoes, Paint Balls . . . and Other Indoor/Outdoor Devotionals You Can Do With Your Kids

Tim Shoemaker

CHRISTIAN PUBLICATIONS, INC.
CAMP HILL, PENNSYLVANIA

Dedication

To Cheryl . . . the one who said "I do" . . . and still does.

And to our Lord, who brought us together and gave us three wonderful sons. All honor goes to the One who never leaves us nor forsakes us, who gives us strength and hope and love.

⊡ CHRISTIAN PUBLICATIONS, INC.
3825 Hartzdale Drive, Camp Hill, PA 17011
www.christianpublications.com

Faithful, biblical publishing since 1883

Mashed Potatoes, Paint Balls . . .
ISBN: 0-87509-977-7
© 2002 by Tim Shoemaker
All rights reserved
Printed in the United States of America

02   03   04   05   06   5   4   3   2   1

Unless otherwise indicated,
Scripture taken from the HOLY BIBLE:
NEW INTERNATIONAL VERSION ®.
Copyright © 1973, 1978, 1984 by the
International Bible Society. Used by
permission of Zondervan Bible Publishers.

NOTE: Italicized words in Scripture quotations
are the emphasis of the author.

Contents

INDOOR DEVOTIONS

Walking with Christ doesn't happen instantly—just as becoming a great musician doesn't happen without practice and effort. You'll illustrate this truth by trying to make music on an instrument you've never played before.

Use a tongue twister to open up a discussion about some other things that are hard to say, such as "I'm sorry" or "I was wrong."

A pocketknife will serve as a reminder about how we should talk to others.

Use a jar of jam to illustrate the appeal of a life unpolluted by worthless things.

The world dupes people into believing that what it has to offer can really satisfy. We're going to expose this illusion—with a bag of marshmallows!

OUTDOOR DEVOTIONS

Foreword

"Tim Shoemaker, where were you when we were raising our kids?"

For almost twenty years, my wife Karen and I have had the privilege of speaking at marriage and parenting conferences across the country. We are often asked, "How do we make family devotions interesting so that our kids stay engaged?" As they ask the question you can see a bit of frustration and even discouragement on some of their faces. Every Christian parent wants the truth of God's Word to capture the hearts and imaginations of their children.

In *Mashed Potatoes, Paint Balls and Other Indoor/Outdoor Devotionals You Can Do With Your Kids*, Tim Shoemaker provides us with a resource that does just that!

As I read the manuscript I found myself eagerly looking forward to what was next. You are holding in your hands a creative, relevant, engaging piece of work. Tim has wrapped truth in compelling word pictures that kids (and moms and dads too!) can readily identify with. If you have been looking for an effective, fun way to pass on life-changing truth to your children, then look no further. Who says devotions have to be boring?

No, this is not a quick fix for the discipline/commitment challenge. No matter how well-written and inviting the resource is, you still have to make the commitment to do it. But it sure is a lot easier when your family is actually looking forward to the experience. Tim has done a wonderful job in helping all of us to have a great time. He even gives us an invaluable set of guidelines on using the book and getting the most out of family devotions. I love it!

Thank you, Tim, for honoring God's truth in such a creative way and for giving us both hope and help as we shape the lives of the next generation. As parents and grandparents, we do not need to feel as if we are failures as the spiritual leaders in our homes. It is my prayer that God will use this important resource to transform many lives. I know He will!

Crawford W. Loritts, Jr.
Associate Director of U.S. Ministries,
Campus Crusade for Christ
Host of daily radio program
"Living the Legacy" on Moody Radio
Husband and father of four

"Hey . . . Buying This Book Wasn't My Idea!"

Is *that* what you're thinking? Soooo. Somebody gave you this book as a not-so-subtle hint that you should be leading family devotions, eh? Don't you hate that?

I know the feeling. Part of you has no intention of reading this book, or any other one on family devotions for that matter. You're not wild about the idea of trying to lead family devotions. You know the routine all too well. Either the kids look totally bored or they simply won't settle down and pay attention. The truth is, family devotions would be a lot easier without the kids, right?

There's another part of you that wishes there was a way to make family devotions work. Deep down you feel the responsibility and a desire to pass on some important truths to the kids. You haven't found an effective way to do that, though, and you're not too anxious to try again.

The good news is that there is a way. It isn't perfect, but this book is what you need. Written in a coaching style, I'll be with you all the way as you sail into the treacherous waters of family devotions.

The devotions in this book are designed to be used once a week and are all based on some activity or object lesson that will engage the kids and actually hold their interest. There's a switch, huh? The activity portion is your ticket to get the kids' attention. The activity naturally leads into a *short* five- or ten-minute devotional that brings home a spiritual truth that is vital for your kids in an evil world. The kids will actually *enjoy* this family time.

Even if you got this book from a well-meaning friend or relative, think about something for a second. What if it was *God* who prompted that person to buy it for you? Whoa. What a thought, eh? That isn't too far-fetched of an idea either. Why *wouldn't* God want you to teach spiritual truths to the kids?

Sometimes you have to do something you hate to protect something you love. You may hate the thought of family devotions, but it's a great way to help protect your kids.

So give it a try. Take the bull by the horns. Read the *How to Use This Book* section, then read through one of the devotions. As you read, you'll find yourself thinking things like, *I can do this*, and *Hey, this looks like fun*, or maybe, *Oh yeah, this is my style*. Now it's time to take this book for a little spin and see what it can *really* do. Try it with the kids.

You're going to enjoy this. I know, because I was in the same boat you're in now. I avoided leading family devotions for the longest time. I tried a lot of things. I stopped and started, and then tried again. These devotions are different. They'll work for you *and* the kids.

Oh, and you know that nagging guilt you try to bury? That voice inside you that accuses you of not doing enough to prepare your kids for life in a fallen world? You'll finally be able to drop-kick that burden right out of your life.

I'm making a lot of promises here, eh? Well, don't take my word on it. Find out for yourself how well these work. You'll never regret giving family devotions one more try.

Not Just for Dads . . .

Sure . . . ideally all family devotions would be led by a dad. That isn't always possible, though. The devoes in this book can effectively be led by a mom or a grandparent. Even an aunt or uncle can use these devoes when the nieces and nephews are over.

They work in groups, too. I've seen youth leaders and Sunday school teachers use these devotions to get a spiritual truth across in an unforgettable way.

So no matter who you are, there's no excuse not to use these devoes to impact kids for Jesus Christ. Come on . . . you can do this!

How to Use This Book

1. *Keep your family devotional time short.* Most of the time there will be some kind of object lesson or activity to do before you actually tie the devotional together with some real teaching. It's OK to extend the activity time if the kids are really enjoying it, but you want to keep your teaching time to about ten minutes. Less is more. You have to resist the tendency to "preach." This is extremely important. If you start going longer, you'll bore the kids. Once they're bored, your job gets a lot tougher. If you keep it short, the kids are less likely to tune you out.

2. *Plan ahead.* These family devoes are designed to be done once a week. The key is to do them well, and that takes a little bit of preparation. Read the devoes for the upcoming week well ahead of time. Sometimes you'll need to pick up some supplies or arrange for some help.

3. *Let the book be your guide.* The parts written in the shaded areas are just for you. That's where I play "coach" to help you through the devotional. And don't think you need to memorize the lesson either. When I'm doing family devoes, I always have my notes in front of me, just like they're written in this book.

4. *Personalize the devotions.* Gear them to the age of your kids. The devoes in this book work pretty well for ages eight to fifteen or so. If your kids are older or younger you may need to make some adjustments. The rest comes down to preparation and persistence. As you read the devotional in advance, you may see some areas where you'd like to slip in a

personal example or one from the news that week. Excellent. That will make your devoes that much better.

5. *Don't let the little problems discourage you*. OK, you *will* get discouraged from time to time, but keep going. It will get better—trust me. If you miss a week, don't beat yourself up over it. Just get back on track as soon as you can. If the kids don't seem to be paying attention, don't be fooled; they hear everything you say. Are they fooling around too much? Don't get upset. Roll with it; join in the fun. It's a sign that they're enjoying devotions—and that's good news!

6. *Hang in there!* I mean it. Family devotions can be tough. But remember, sometimes you have to do something you hate to protect something you love. You love your kids and you need to protect them by helping them prepare for the battles of life. One way you do this is by teaching them in family devotional time.

As time goes on, you'll find that family devoes aren't so hard after all. You'll find the kids will really enjoy them, even look forward to them. The best thing is that you'll be helping them prepare for life in some areas that are really important. You'll never regret the effort you make to have family devotions.

I'm encouraging you to do something good for your kids—and for yourself as well. And you'll probably shock the person who gave you this book while you're at it!

C'mon. Give this book a try. You can do it!

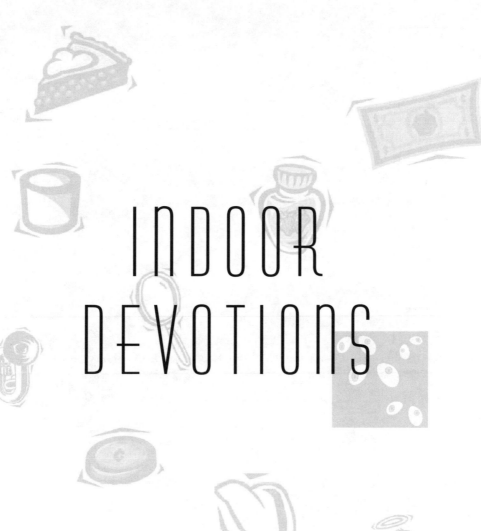

INDOOR DEVOTIONS

Practice Makes Perfect

What's the Point?

Walking with Christ doesn't happen instantly—just as becoming a great musician doesn't happen without practice and effort. You'll illustrate this truth by trying to make music on an instrument you've never played before.

Things You'll Need:

- An instrument

You'll need an instrument that you absolutely don't know how to play. (For most of us, that shouldn't be too hard to find!) Check with friends or relatives for an instrument you can borrow— something that's pretty hard to play, like a guitar, violin, tuba, whatever. (Sorry, a kazoo won't do.) You're going to play this instrument for the kids, and the worse you sound, the better. Some sheet music would come in handy—just to make it look good.

Here We Go

Pull out the instrument and the music and tell the kids something like this:

I'm sure you're surprised to see me with this instrument. You probably didn't even know I could play it. Well, I'd like you to sit back, relax and enjoy a little number I'm going to play for you.

Begin playing your horrible, unrecognizable tune, despite their howling protests. When you're finished, get some feedback.

OK. Tell me what you think. In fact, rank me from one to ten. One would mean I was very bad, ten would mean I was excellent.

Get their input. If they're ranking you around zero, it will be music to your ears (pardon the pun). Now you need to go a bit further.

What would you say if I told you that I considered myself to be a musician with this instrument? What if I told you that I truly believed I could pick up this instrument anytime I wanted and play like a pro even though I never took lessons?

Again, get their feedback. It should run along the lines of "You're nuts!" If that's the general way the kids are responding, you've done a great job. They're wide open for a dose of the truth.

8

All right, all right. I get the picture. Let me read you some verses from the Bible.

> *Flee* the evil desires of youth, and *pursue* righteousness, faith, love and peace. (2 Timothy 2:22)

> Our people must *learn* to *devote* themselves to *doing* what is good, in order that they may . . . not live unproductive lives. (Titus 3:14)

> Whatever happens, *conduct* yourselves in a manner worthy of the gospel of Christ. (Philippians 1:27)

> Continue to *work* out your salvation. . . . (2:12)

Did you notice that all these verses talk about how being an effective Christian takes work, practice and self-discipline? God never intended for us to become "saved" and then never work at becoming more like Jesus.

Tie It Together

If I were truly considered a musician on this instrument, I'd be able to play real music. Now, if I really wanted to be good at this instrument, what would I have to do?

Get ready for a sarcastic response. After your little recital, they'll probably see you as a hopeless case! That's OK. Hopefully they'll eventually suggest you get some lessons.

Yeah, I'll never be good at this instrument unless I put some effort into it. I'd need to take lessons and practice my heart out.

It's the same way with being a Christian. Living like a Christian doesn't come naturally. You just can't live the Christian life without some lessons and practice. How can I get lessons on how to be a good Christian, a follower of Christ?

See what they say here. You'll probably get answers like, "Go to church," "Read your Bible" or something similar. That's good. There's also learning from the example of others, good or bad. They have the idea. We just need them to see that hearing isn't enough, they have to practice. They have to discipline themselves.

For a lot of Christians, the only "lessons" they get for living a genuine Christian life come from church. The problem is that they don't actively try to apply what they've learned there to their own personal life. They rarely try putting anything they might happen to learn from the Bible into practice.

Hey, I'm not much of a "musician" on this instrument because I've never practiced it before. In the same way, I wouldn't be a very good example of a genuine Christian if I didn't work at it.

How can I practice what I learn at church and in family devotions so that thinking and acting like a Christian will come easier for me?

Let them think here. How *do* they do that? How do you do it in your life? You need to think this through before you ask them.

You know, some Christians don't want to put any effort into growing as a Christian at all. They think that they can just call on God when they really need Him, like when they're in a jam.

The problem is, when you ask for help, you need to trust God. Having faith can be tough—it takes a lot of practice. When you're in the middle of a mess, it's usually too late to start "taking lessons" on trusting God.

What if I only *read* the music, but never practiced? I still wouldn't be much of a musician, would I? Just *reading* the Bible isn't enough. If you never try to put what you read into practice, you won't grow as a Christian either.

OK, we've been hitting them with a pretty heavy concept here. Time to back off a little and change gears. Now give *them* a chance with the instrument. Let them follow the music and play a song. They'll probably be as bad at it as you were. Then take the instrument back and give them a quick wrap-up.

We want to be good Christians. We want to be effective Christians—followers of Christ. We can't just make that happen instantly, any more than we can be instant

musicians. We've got to work at it every day. How can you work on it this week?

Get some brief input or give them some practical applications yourself if they get stuck. You may even want to keep that instrument around for a while as a reminder.

A soldier must practice and gain skills with weapons and fighting tactics before he goes to battle. Can you imagine a marine in the middle of a battle sitting in a foxhole trying to read an instruction manual for his gun? That's crazy!

As Christians, we do that all the time. We coast along and don't prepare for the battles to come. We don't strengthen our walk with the Lord or our faith in Him. Those are the things we need to draw on when we face the tough times.

When hard times come, we're like that marine in a foxhole—helpless. We're an easy target for the enemy and no real help to others around us either.

Let's work on that, OK? Being a good musician takes practice. Living a genuine, productive Christian life takes work and practice too.

This devotional is a good reminder for all of us, isn't it? Keep it up!

Tongue Twisters

What's the Point?

Use a tongue twister to open up a discussion about some other things that are hard to say, such as "I'm sorry" or "I was wrong."

Things You'll Need

- A book of tongue twisters

You can pick up a book of tongue twisters at the local library. Don't worry if the book is geared for a younger age level. This is one time you can get away with it. You could even use the children's classic, Oh Say, Can You Say? *(Random House, 1979) by Theodor Seuss Geisel, otherwise known as Dr. Seuss.*

I've got one of my own tongue twisters if you don't have any luck finding others. Anyway, you can do this devotional almost anywhere.

Here We Go

Gather the kids for family devoes, grab your tongue twisters book and challenge them to read one you've selected. Make them read it out loud as fast as they can. You may want to time them and compete to see who can say it the fastest. (Include yourself in the competition—but it's no fair practicing ahead of time and having an unfair advantage!) If you didn't find a book at the library, here's one tongue twister you can use:

How about a black bass sax from Jack's Black Bass Sax Shack? I'll bet they have a whole pack of black bass saxes in the back racks of Jack's Black Bass Sax Shack!

How did they do? If they didn't stumble as they read, make them do it again, but faster this time. If you really want to make them look foolish, have them say it several times in a row. Speed is the key here.

If you have any other tongue twisters, have them try out those as well and see how they do. After you've had some fun with this, move on before the idea gets old and the kids get bored. You might say something like this:

OK, so tongue twisters are a good example of things that are hard to say. I've got a list of some other phrases that are even harder to say. Anybody want to read my list?

If you have a volunteer, great—it keeps them involved. If not, just go ahead and read it. Customize the list for your family if you need to. If you're the one reading it, glance up after every line to see their reactions. Here's the list:

I'm sorry.

It was my fault.

Would you forgive me?

I appreciate you.

I love you.

What can I do to help you?

OK, now they're getting an idea of where you're going. You might even catch a smile or two.

Now, it's easy to see why a tongue twister is so hard to say, but what is it about this list of phrases we just read that makes *them* so difficult to say?

Let's see if they give you a response here. If not, try this question:

Which of these do you think is the hardest for people to say?

Listen up—they may just reveal the one that they struggle with the most.

What makes it so hard?

I know, I know. You're doing a lot of probing here. Hey, if it works, great. If they clam up and begin to look uncomfortable, you'd better move on. The key is, they *are* thinking. Count on it.

I'd say it comes down to pride an awful lot. We hate to admit we were wrong, even a little bit. Sometimes we hate to admit we need other people. Here are a few Bible verses:

A gentle tongue can break a bone. (Proverbs 25:15)

Therefore confess your sins to each other and pray for each other so that you may be healed. (James 5:16)

A gentle answer turns away wrath, but a harsh word stirs up anger. (Proverbs 15:1)

Tie It Together

While it isn't exactly easy or comfortable to say things like "I'm sorry" or "I was wrong," we need to do it. Just like a tongue twister, the more we work at it, the easier it gets to say it.

If I avoid saying things like "I'm sorry," I've probably got a pride problem. Pride is a sinister sin. It is so subtle, often we don't even notice it's there. We think pride is harmless, but the truth is that pride will hurt us in many ways. If God has a list of the sins He hates most, pride has to be in the top three, if not number one. After all, pride is the reason for Satan's fall.

One verse I read a minute ago talked about our need to confess to each other when we're wrong. It's often harder to say than a tongue twister, but we need to do it. We need to be able to say we're sorry and really mean it when we do.

The last verse pointed out how powerful it can be when we speak in a kind way. Expressing appreciation or love for those close to you, and yes, confessing humbly when we're wrong can be much more powerful than we might guess.

OK, you've been doing all the talking. Now wrap it up and end it pronto.

Let me read you one more verse. It makes a nice prayer to God, asking for His help when it comes to the things that come out of your mouth.

> Set a guard over my mouth, O LORD; keep watch over the door of my lips. (Psalm 141:3)

Remember that list:

I'm sorry.

It was my fault.

Would you forgive me?

I appreciate you.

I love you.

What can I do to help you?

These are some pretty tough things to say at times. But just like a tongue twister, the more we say them, the easier it will get. Let's all work on it, OK?

Pocketknife

What's the Point?

A pocketknife will serve as a reminder about how we should talk to others.

Things You'll Need:

- A small pocketknife (or even one for each kid)
- A small, sturdy cardboard box
- A snack that will fit in the box such as candy, soda, etc.
- A roll of heavy-duty tape (gentlemen, break out your duct tape!)

My blade of choice is a "Buck" brand pocketknife. (No, it doesn't have to be a "Buck" brand; it's just that the name "Buck" stamped on the knife will come in real handy later on.) This would be a great devotional to do while camping, by the way.

If you can get one knife for each person, it will really help them remember this lesson. I was fortunate to find a very small-bladed "Buck" knife really cheap; it worked perfectly for the devotions.

Put your goodies inside the cardboard box and seal it up with the tape, wrapping it around and around the box.

Here We Go

Get the kids together for devotions. Keep the box in plain sight but the pocketknife hidden in your pocket for now. You might start out saying something like this.

I've got this box here, and I'll bet you're wondering exactly what's inside, right? Anybody want to open it?

Now, you'll probably have some volunteers here. If someone gets the brainy idea to use a knife or scissors, tell them you want them to try doing it with their bare hands first. If anybody tries to get too physical with the box, great! It fits in with the devotional. But let them know that there's something inside you want to share with them, so they probably don't want it ruined.

Watch them struggle a little, then take the box away and talk with them a bit.

OK, so this box isn't quite as easy to open as you might have hoped. I put quite a bit of tape around it. Let me share a couple of verses with you.

A gentle answer turns away wrath, but a harsh word stirs up anger. (Proverbs 15:1)

For as churning the milk produces butter, and as twisting the nose produces blood, so stirring up anger produces strife. (30:33)

The tongue . . . is a fire, a world of evil among the parts of the body. It corrupts the whole person, sets the whole course of his life on fire, and is itself set on fire by hell. (James 3:6)

There are a ton of other verses I could share. I'm thinking about how we talk when it comes to relating to other people. Can somebody put the main point of these verses in their own words?

This is a real shot in the dark. You may get nothing but blank stares. No problemo. If they do have some input, great, but don't be disappointed if they don't. Take whatever they give you and move on.

Sometimes when we relate to others, we try to force things to go our own way: We argue, we insult, we intimidate. It's like trying to get into the box with our bare hands. It can be tough, and we struggle with it. If we struggle too much, we're going to damage what's inside the box.

Sometimes we hurt people around us because of the way we talk to them. Just like this box covered with tape, they resist you. Does anybody have an example of when harsh words made relating with someone harder?

Let them think a little here. If they aren't coming up with anything, try rephrasing the question. "Can you think of a time that someone wanted something from you, but the way they spoke to you made you want to resist them?" (Fair warning here: The person they have in mind may be you!)

You want this box to be impossible to open without the trusty knife. Use some packing material, so the snacks won't rattle around in there and spoil the surprise.

Avoiding the ER

I know, I know—knives can be dangerous, so just be careful. (Let's face it, any kid who ever owned a pocketknife ended up with a cut sooner or later. I'd keep a couple of little bandages handy.)

If you're ready to be open to some criticism, go ahead and ask, "Have I ever treated you that way?" This may be an excellent opportunity to deal with this. It may be your chance to see how you and your kids could relate better to each other.

If they aren't coming up with anything, and you're a little nervous about setting yourself up as a target, be ready with a story you can share—preferably from your own childhood—about how someone's way of talking to you made you want to shut them out. Keep it short.

That's what some of these verses are trying to point out. Harsh words, intimidating or insulting talk don't exactly make people want to open up to you. They create barriers, not bridges. Let me share another verse with you.

> Through patience a ruler can be persuaded, and a gentle tongue can break a bone. (Proverbs 25:15)

I love this verse. "A gentle tongue can break a bone." What does this mean to you?

Let's see what they say here. They're getting the picture, you can be sure of that. They may not be ready to share their thoughts yet. If not, move on.

Tie It Together

The Bible tells us we'll be a lot more effective with people if we are patient with them. If we speak gently to them, we're much more

likely to make a real impact. We need to be understanding, caring and kind when we relate to others.

That was a key line, by the way. If you got the "Buck" brand knives, you'll use the word "Buck" as an acronym. Be Understanding, Caring & Kind.

I can struggle with other people (*struggle with the tape on the box with bare hands*) or I can be understanding, caring and kind. I've got this little pocketknife here (*pull it out of your pocket*). Let's say it represents being gentle with others like the verse said.

Pull out the blade and slice through the tape. Since this is supposed to represent gentleness, don't struggle to cut the box open. Do it leisurely; make it look effortless. In other words, make sure the knife is sharp!

Presto. Check out what's inside.

Pass the box to the kids and let them enjoy the treats.

I did the wrap job on this box in a way that made it pretty tough to open without the right tool. God has designed people to relate to each other better when they follow His principles for doing it.

Yeah, just like it was a lot easier to open up the box with a little pocketknife, people will respond much better to you when you watch how you talk to them.

When you intimidate, argue and insult people, they're a lot less likely to really open up to you. Instead, let's work on being gentle. Let's be understanding, caring and kind. You'll be a lot more effective with people if you are.

If you have a little "Buck" knife for each of them, now is the time to pull them out. You might say something like this:

I have a little pocketknife for each of you. Notice the brand name? (*Point to each letter as you say the next line.*) B̲c U̲nderstanding, C̲aring & K̲ind. I'm hoping this will be a little reminder to help you keep that in mind when you're talking to other people.

You might close in prayer. You may also want to think through how you talk to the kids. Maybe you need to ask their forgiveness. Ask God to help each of you work on it.

One more thing: If you give them knives, be sure to go over some safety tips and ground rules, like not bringing it to school, etc. (Their principal may not understand when they explain that they carry a pocketknife to help them remember to be kind to others!)

Pure Preserves

What's the Point?

Use a jar of jam to illustrate the appeal of a life unpolluted by worthless things.

Things You'll Need

- Two fresh jars of strawberry preserves (find a brand with the word "preserves" on the label instead of "jam"—this is important)
- A spoon and a plate or bowl, other than the ones you and the kids will use (trust me, you won't want to eat off these dishes by the time we're done!)
- Some fresh rolls or toast to put the jam on (or ice cream, if you think the kids would appreciate that more)
- A handful of dirty coins, in a clear sandwich bag (make sure they look totally gross; be sure to put a little dirt or pet hair in the bag along with the coins)

Here We Go

Tell the kids something like this:

I have a couple of jars of jam here. Sometimes jam is called "preserves." Why? Because the jam is kept fresh, or "preserved" in a jar.

Open one jar and scoop out a couple of big heaps onto a plate or into a bowl.

Now here's a scoop of jam or preserves that you probably think looks pretty good. What would you think if I took this bag of dirty change and mixed it into the jam?

Actually toss the dirt and coins in and stir. Let the kids have a good look at it as you move on. You want to gross them out a little.

Oh, yeah. These coins have been all over. In fact (*with a smile*) I picked up these coins on the bathroom floor of a gas station on the way home today.

Scoop up a spoonful of jam with a coin or two in it and hold it out to the kids.

Anybody want a spoonful?

Any normal person should say "no thanks" to your offer, but we're talking about kids here, so don't be surprised if you have a volunteer. Just roll with their response—but I wouldn't be letting anyone do a taste test!

Most people would say "no thanks" to my offer to taste this. I wouldn't want it either.

This is a scoop of *polluted* jam. It isn't *pure* preserves like this other jar here. Let me read you a Bible verse.

> Turn my eyes away from worthless things; *preserve* my life according to your word. (Psalm 119:37)

Tie It Together

A jar of jam, or "preserves," is a lot like our life. God doesn't want us to fill our life with a lot of worthless things that will pollute us in some way.

What kinds of worthless things can we put in our life?

Get their feedback . . . it will vary depending on their age, etc. Don't stop at just a list of the more obvious answers. Prompt them to list attitudes that are worthless and pollute us as well, such as pride, selfishness, complaining, etc.

God wants our life to be pure. He wants to enjoy us like you or I would enjoy some really fresh preserves. He wants us to be appetizing for others. In other words, a Christian should look so appealing to others that they desire what we have: Christ in our life.

According to that verse I read, we need to live in agreement with God's Word. What's that mean? (*Give them a chance to respond.*) It means we need to *obey* God's Word. It also means we need to stay away from things the

Bible tells us to avoid. We need to pursue the things the Bible says we should pursue. Can you think of any examples?

Be sure to get really practical here. If they say, "by loving each other," ask how we can do that. Other ways to live in agreement with God's Word could involve not complaining or arguing (Philippians 2:14), being content with what we have (Hebrews 13:5) and, of course, learning to resist our natural pride and selfishness. You want to get the kids thinking, but don't take a long time on this. You'll bore them to tears.

OK, now it's time to show 'em just how good pure preserves can be. Break out the rolls or ice cream, open that fresh jar of preserves and heap some on for the kids. You'll want to set a good example and take a healthy portion for yourself as well (it's a tough job, but somebody's got to do it!).

As they're enjoying the snack, ask them how they like it. You should get some very positive feedback. Close by saying something like this:

The reason it's so good is that the preserves are fresh and pure, not polluted with things that don't belong there. If you keep your life unpolluted, if you keep it in agreement with God's Word, you'll have a life that will be just as appealing to God and others as that snack was to you.

The Houdini Principle

What's the Point?

The world dupes people into believing that what it has to offer can really satisfy. We're going to expose this illusion—with a bag of marshmallows!

Things You'll Need

Hey, this one is easy, but you'll need to start working on this a week or so ahead of the date you plan to have family devoes. First, get a bag of marshmallows. (I prefer the big, fluffy kind, like the ones I used to throw to the polar bears at the zoo when I was a kid.)

Put the bag of marshmallows in a box and wrap it up nice. You may want to put some weight in it so the box doesn't feel empty. Keep the box in plain sight of the whole family all week. Let the kids know the package is for them and that they can open it when you have devotions later in the week.

Now to build their anticipation for the package all week. If they quiz you about what's in the package, be vague but encouraging. ("You're gonna love it. Sorry, you'll have to wait.")

But don't stop there— build the kids' excitement

Here We Go

If you haven't built some real anticipation in the kids' minds about opening the package, stall a couple of days until you do. Excitement and anticipation are the keys to driving the point of the devoes home.

If you *have* built some excitement, great! Keep the momentum going as you start devoes. Here's where the camera and/or video recorder comes in. You'll want to pull it out so you can get pictures as the kids open it up. This act alone may clinch it in their minds. They're about to get something *really* good.

OK, tell them to open the package. Snap a picture as they start ripping into it. Snap another as they pull out the bag of jumbo marshmallows. They're going to feel a little foolish as they realize the package wasn't nearly as great as they'd expected. They may even feel just a little bit deceived by you. That will work just fine for our purposes.

Hey, marshmallows! Wow, what a surprise, huh?

They'll definitely agree, but they won't be too happy about it. They may start complaining at this point. If so, listen to their complaints and then keep going.

OK. I understand your disappointment. You had every reason to think you were really getting something good. Let me read you a couple of verses. Then we'll make some sense of all this.

Do not store up for yourselves treasures on earth, where moth and rust destroy, and where thieves break in and steal. But store up for yourselves treasures in heaven, where moth and rust do not destroy, and where thieves do not break in and steal. For where your treasure is, there your heart will be also. (Matthew 6:19-21)

Tie It Together

This whole week we've been telling you about the package—our excitement, the phone message from _____, the camera—all these things led you to believe that what you were going to get was going to make you really happy.

That's a lot like life. We're surrounded by advertising for all kinds of products that promise to make us happy, to make life worthwhile. These advertisements were designed by people who get paid unbelievable sums of money to make their product appear to be able to deliver real satisfaction to our lives. The truth is, they're good at it.

Plenty of people think they could be truly happy if they achieved a certain weight, if they owned a certain car, drank a particular beverage or simply made enough money.

It's all an illusion. Harry Houdini never performed an illusion that was more convincing than what the advertisers pull off in our culture every day.

even more. Here's one idea: Have a relative (a grandparent, aunt or uncle) call—preferably when they know you're not home, so they can leave this message on your phone answering machine: "Hi, [name]. Your parents told me about the package they have planned for you this week. I'm so happy for you. Congratulations." Or, "I heard about the package your parents are giving you this weekend. You are so lucky! My parents never did anything like that for me."

Add a note or card in the mail from some friend of the family along the same lines. If the kids get a few messages like this during the week, they'll really begin to think there's something mighty special in the package. That's perfect. This is going to be fun.

By this time, the kids will truly believe the gift is going to be great, or they'll be very suspicious. In either case, they'll be looking forward to family devotions to find out what this is all about. That's good. So have fun with this during the week. This is a classic case of selling the "sizzle" instead of the steak.

One more thing. Have the camera loaded with film for devotions. A video camera would be good too.

Some people chase after happiness and contentment their entire lives, but never really find it—or, at least not for long. The problem is that they've been fooled into looking for it in the wrong places. They think that if they get a good enough job to make enough money so they can buy the right things, they'll be happy. It's the Houdini principle, and it is one very convincing illusion.

I'll give you a clue as to why it's so convincing. The whole Houdini principle was designed by the father of lies himself—the devil, the master of deception. If he can get people to think that they can achieve lasting happiness, contentment and satisfaction from the things they can buy, he wins a major victory. Why would that be so important?

We've been talking quite a bit here. Let's see if they're tracking with us. Give them a moment to respond, then close with this:

If the devil can get people to believe that they can make it on their own, that money and things will make them happy, he gets them distracted. He gets them to go down the wrong road. He keeps them from finding out that only God can give us lasting happiness, contentment and satisfaction. Some guys spend their whole lives climbing to the top, only to find out when they get there that they've been climbing the wrong mountain.

The devil is so powerfully convincing, he makes one of Houdini's performances look like amateur night. Houdini was out to entertain audiences with his illusions. The devil is out to destroy people with his.

The package you opened was filled with marshmallows—a bag of fluff! Pretty disappointing, huh? The same thing can happen to you in life if you're not careful. If you buy into the devil's lies, you'll get nothing but "fluff" instead of lasting happiness.

Now break open that bag. I'm hungry!

Worse than a Bad Tattoo

What's the Point?

A silly temporary tattoo will get the kids thinking about living a lifetime with something much worse—regret.

Things You'll Need

- A bunch of temporary tattoos—the type you apply with a moist cloth (If you really want to drive home the point of this devotional, select tattoos that your kids would be embarrassed to be seen wearing. Have some fun with this.)
- One moist cloth for each of the kids. While one of the kids holds the cloth on their tattoo, you can be working on the next one.

Here We Go

Get your kids together along with the tattoos and moist cloths. I wouldn't let the kids see the tattoos at first. You might pick one of the older kids to be your helper.

The person getting the tattoos holds out their arm and closes their eyes. Next, you put a tattoo on their forearm and cover it with the wet cloth. You may want to apply more than one tattoo to each person's forearm. Then have them hold the moist cloth on it so they can't see it while you tattoo your next victim. Ideally, nobody will see their tattoos until you're done with every one of the kids. If you used a helper, you'll probably want to tattoo them too.

Now go back and peel off the backing for each person's tattoo and let them see your "masterpiece." You might proceed with something like this:

Nice surprise, huh? Does everybody like their tattoos?

If the kids think the tattoos you've applied are really great, it may be a little harder to get the lesson across. Hopefully they are semi-horrified at the selection of tattoos you've emblazoned on their forearms. They may even be wanting to wash the tattoos off. That would be a perfect reaction.

Oh, so you're not so happy with my choices for you, eh? The good news is that these are temporary. They fade away in a week or two.

If you got some really lousy tattoos, you should hear some howling protests at this point. Of course, that line about "a week or two" is a bunch of baloney, but it's good to get them thinking about being stuck with the tattoo for a while.

No, the truth is we can wash these off any time we want, with some good scrubbing anyway. Think about something, though: What if it was permanent? What if this could *never* be removed? Can you imagine being stuck with tattoos like this for the rest of your life?

Pause for a reaction. It may be a face they make, or you may get a comment. That's fine. Keep rolling.

I know what you mean. If the tattoo was permanent, that would be awful, wouldn't it? I know something that's even worse than a bad-looking tattoo. Like a real tattoo, it stays around for life. Like a real tattoo, you can cover it up, but it's still there. You can't get rid of it. Any idea of what I'm talking about?

Give them a chance to guess. They've been trying to figure it out anyway. They probably won't guess exactly what we're looking for, but their answers may be interesting.

I could be talking about a lot of things, but the one I had in mind is regret. That's right, regret. Sound strange? Regret is a real fooler that way. Regret can cripple you, change

"When I Was Your Age . . ."

Think back on a decision you made, or something you did that you regret to this day. How has it impacted you? How has it held you back? You may want to share that with the kids during the devotional. If you can think of something you did when you were their age, all the better.

The flip side to that is to think of something that you did or said a long time ago that you don't regret. It may be something you almost didn't do, something you would have regretted if you hadn't done the right thing. Hopefully you'll have a chance to share this too.

you, hold you back. What are some things that kids do that they may regret later?

Big question. We didn't ask them what *they* do that they may regret someday, but what *others* may do; it's a little less intimidating that way. Listen carefully, though—they may give you some clues as to what they're struggling with. Take what they give you and round it out with your own list.

There are all kinds of things we can regret. It might be something we say or do. It may be something we've done wrong. Even if nobody ever finds out, the regret is there, just like a tattoo hidden by a sleeve.

It may be something we fail to do. We miss an opportunity to say or do something and then *BOOM!* It's with us the rest of our lives, in the form of a regret.

Tie It Together

There are plenty of examples in the Bible of people who suffered from regrets. How about Samson? He chased after the wrong girl. He knew she wasn't the right kind of girl for him, but he went after her anyway. After all, he was the strongest man in the world! His superhuman strength had gotten him out of plenty of jams before, so he figured he could handle this situation too.

He was wrong, of course; his bad choices came back to haunt him. The girl betrayed him, his enemies captured him and the soldiers gouged his eyes out so he could not escape. He would never walk as a free man again. Think he had regrets?

> They may respond, but don't sweat it if they don't. The story of Samson is so powerful, they may just be quiet and thinking.

Oh yeah, he had regrets all right. They haunted him every day. His enemies made him a slave, giving him work normally assigned to donkeys.

How about David? Do you think he ever regretted his decision to commit adultery? You don't have to read far in Psalm 51 to pick up on that. Listen to some of the things he says:

> Have mercy on me, O God . . .
> Blot out my transgressions. Wash away all my iniquity and cleanse me from my sin.
> My sin is always before me.
> Cleanse me . . .
> Wash me . . .
> Save me . . .

Get the picture? Regret is a horrible thing. We can let it consume us until we can't do the things we should, which only leads to more regret. It can hold us back and weigh us down; it's with us the rest of our lives.

God forgives, of course; He forgave David, and He forgave Samson. But the regret is still there. David wished he'd never sinned; Sam-

son wished he'd not compromised. Like a bad tattoo, regret is permanent even after you receive forgiveness.

This would be a good time to share a regret that you have or maybe of someone you know. We need to bring this lesson to the kid's world. It needs to be closer to home. Share your heart with them.

How much better to never have the regret in the first place. Think of the disciples who followed when Jesus called—no regrets there! How about Shadrach and his buddies in the fiery furnace, or Daniel in the lion's den? No regrets there either.

Got a story you can share about something you said or did and now that you look back on it, you're really happy that you did? This would be a great time to share it.

I've done some things that I regret to this day. There were other times I *could* have done something I would have regretted, but I did the right thing instead. I'm so glad I did.

As a parent, I want you to be wise. I want you to avoid the obvious wrong choices, the compromises, the careless things you may say or do. I don't want you to live with the pain of regret. It can keep us from being free to be everything God wants us to be. Don't dare take it lightly.

In the Bible, Solomon is described as the wisest man who ever lived. The book of Proverbs is a collection of wisdom that God wanted him to pass on to us. Proverbs warns over and over again about being very careful about the things we do and the choices we make. It describes the consequences too.

Solomon urges young people to listen to what he has to say. He encourages them to do the right things and avoid the consequences of doing wrong. One of the consequences is regret. Listen to a few things Solomon said:

> I guide you in the way of wisdom and lead you along straight paths. When you walk, your steps will not be hampered; when you run, you will not stumble. Hold on to instruction, do not let it go; guard it well, for it is your life. Do not set foot on the path of the wicked or walk in the way of evil men. Avoid it, do not travel on it; turn from it and go on your way. (Proverbs 4:11-15)

> My son, pay attention to what I say; listen closely to my words. Do not let them out of your sight, keep them within your heart; for they are life to those who find them and health to a man's whole body. Above all else, guard your heart, for it is the wellspring of life. (4:20-23)

> Do not swerve to the right or the left; keep your foot from evil. (4:27)

> Remember your Creator in the days of your youth. (Ecclesiastes 12:1)

Fear God and keep his commandments, for this is the whole duty of man. For God will bring every deed into judgment, including every hidden thing, whether it is good or evil. (Ecclesiastes 12:13-14)

I know, I know. We had a lot of verses here. It's a pretty important topic, and I hate to stop just now, but we don't want to go too long. Let's wrap it up.

Regrets: They're powerful—a lot worse than a bad tattoo. They don't go away, even though you may be forgiven. Before you act, be sure the thing you're going to say or do is something a Christian would be proud or honored to do or say. You can't do it alone. Ask God to help you so you can live with no regrets.

The Trouble with Susan B.

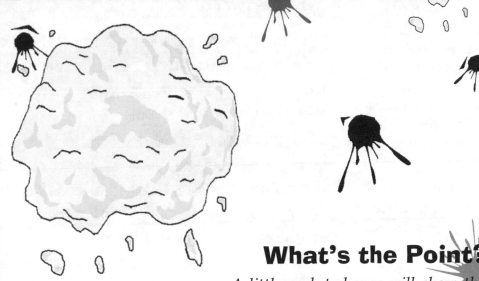

What's the Point?

A little pocket change will show that living too much like the world puts us in danger of losing our true value as Christians.

Things You'll Need

- You'll need a quarter, an old silver dollar and a couple of Susan B. Anthony silver dollars. If you're having any trouble finding the last two, talk to some of your friends at work or at church. Somebody will probably have some squirreled away that you can borrow.

If that doesn't work, try a coin shop. A Susan B. will be cheap. Even a silver dollar will be cheap if you ask for one that's pretty beat up. Be sure the silver dollar is the older type, without the copper center. One from the 1920s is perfect. To emphasize the point of this devotional even more with the kids, get a silver dollar for each of them to keep.

- Finally, you'll need some extra change. You'll want to keep the miscellaneous change in one pocket. Be sure there are at

Here We Go

Get the kids together and sit them down someplace. Pull out all the loose change from your pocket and put it on the table in front of them. Keep all the dollar coins out of sight, but make sure the two Susan Bs are handy so you can slip them out of your other pocket without being obvious. Ask for a volunteer to help you with the change.

Get your volunteer and instruct them to hold both hands out with their palms facing upward. With their eyes closed, put a coin in each hand. Tell them to close their fists tight, keep their eyes closed and guess what kind of coin is in each hand.

Your ultimate intent, as you may have figured out by now, is to fool them by putting a Susan B. in one hand and a quarter in the other; they're practically impossible to tell apart without looking at them. If you want to draw this out a little, start by putting a nickel in one hand and a dime in the other, and giving everyone a chance to try it. On the other hand (pun intended), you may want to do the Susan Bs right away, before the kids begin to suspect you have some kind of trick up your sleeve.

When you're ready to do the Susan Bs, be sure to make a little noise with the change on the table each time before you place a Susan B. in their hand. This way it sounds like you're picking up coins from the table. If this works right, your volunteer will guess that they have quarters in both hands. Congratulations, Houdini! You just pulled off a nice illusion. If it bombs, well, hey, don't worry about it. You can still explain that the Susan B. often fools people less brilliant than your volunteer.

I'm going to assume you pulled it off and that your volunteer thinks both coins are quarters. Now say,

Open your eyes and hands and see if you're right!

Hopefully, you'll catch them by surprise when they see Susan B. staring up at them instead of George Washington. But don't expect a pat on the back—"Gee, Dad, you really had me fooled. That was cool!" No, you'll probably get a reaction more along the lines of, "Hey, that wasn't fair! You didn't have these on the table to begin with." Being a parent can be a thankless job! Anyway, you might say something like this:

That's right—these aren't quarters. They're dollars. The trouble with Susan B. Anthony dollars is that they can be mistaken for quarters so easily. In fact, a lot people have made the same mistake. They've pulled out a Susan B. and used it to pay for something, thinking it was only a quarter. People got so disgusted with poor Susan B. that they've actually stopped making them.

Let me show you something.

Pull out the old silver dollar and place it on the table next to a quarter and the Susan B.

This is an old-style silver dollar. The Susan B. is supposed to be a dollar too—what's the problem here?

least a couple of quarters in there along with some nickels, pennies and dimes. Keep the Susan Bs and the silver dollars in the other pocket.

Try for a little input here. We're hoping they say how similar the Susan B. is to the quarter.

Yeah, the Susan B. looks a lot more like a quarter than a dollar. That happens in life too. A lot of Christians are like Susan B. Anthony dollars. They're silver dollars acting like quarters. Let me read you some verses and tell you what I mean.

There are a bunch of verses here; you may want to pick and choose which ones to read.

Religion that God our Father accepts as pure and faultless is this: to look after orphans and widows in their distress and to keep oneself from being polluted by the world. (James 1:27)

For the grace of God that brings salvation has appeared to all men. It teaches us to say "No" to ungodliness and worldly passions, and to live self-controlled, upright and godly lives in this present age, while we wait for the blessed hope—the glorious appearing of our great God and Savior, Jesus Christ, who gave himself for us to redeem us from all wickedness and to purify for himself a people that are his very own, eager to do what is good. (Titus 2:11-14)

Do not love the world or anything in the world. If anyone loves the world, the love of the Father is not in him. For everything in the world—the cravings of sinful man, the lust of his eyes and the boasting of what he has and does—comes not from the Father but from the world. The world and its desires pass away, but the man who does the will of God lives forever. (1 John 2:15-17)

Set your minds on things above, not on earthly things. (Colossians 3:2)

You adulterous people, don't you know that friendship with the world is hatred toward God? Anyone who chooses to be a friend of the world becomes an enemy of God. (James 4:4)

Do not conform any longer to the pattern of this world, but be transformed by the renewing of your mind. Then you will be able to test and approve what God's will is—his good, pleasing and perfect will. (Romans 12:2)

Tie It Together

OK, let's say Christians are silver dollars, and people who don't know Christ are quarters. The Bible tells us to be different from the world for a couple of reasons: First, we are God's children. We're children of the King and we shouldn't act in a way that would shame the Lord's name. For example, let's say you acted in a really selfish way. Somebody might say, "Hey, look what you did, and you call yourself a Christian?" Your actions dishonor the title "Christian."

Next, the world is lost. It is on the "broad road that leads to destruction," the Bible tells us. If we have the answer to eternal life, then we ought to live differently. We can't just live the same way everyone else does. People have to see there is something different about us. God wants us to be set apart for Him. That's called being holy.

I'll give you one more reason. If I act and live just like everyone who is lost, there's a danger that I might drift away from the Lord.

This is an issue that believers have struggled with for a long time. Years ago, some Christians were trying hard not to live the Christian life as if it were just a list of "do's and don'ts." Their motive was good, because God wants our relationship with Him to be more than "do this and don't do that."

They created a new problem, though. Some Christians began to think they could do just about anything they felt like doing as long as they were "responsible" with how they did it (whatever that means). That kind of thinking can easily become a dangerous twist of the truth. It can lead to Christians who don't think, act or live much different than a non-Christian. As a result, we have a bunch of "Susan B." Christians out there. They're dollars—children of the King—but they act like any other quarter on the street.

Now, I'm not saying we go back to a list of "do's and don'ts," but we *do* need to live lives that are different from people who are lost. Instead of trying to see how close we can be to the world, we need to see how we can look more like Christ.

Hold the quarter, the silver dollar and the Susan B. up so they can see the edges of them. You should notice the big silver dollar is solid silver. The quarter and the Susan B. have a different colored center. Ask them what they see.

OK, when I hold these up, what do you see on the edge? What's different about what makes up the center of them? Yeah, at the very center, at the heart of the coins you see a difference. The quarter and the Susan B. have a copper center. The heart of the big silver dollar is pure silver.

It's the same with being an effective Christian. The key is and always has been the heart. If my relationship with the Lord is real and strong inside, it will naturally affect how I live on the outside.

OK, I admit it. This has gotten long and preachy. Even now, I'm tempted to add a lot more to get this point across, but that would be too much for one sitting. You've said enough to get your kids thinking. Now, like with so many other things, you'll want to reinforce this truth in the course of everyday life in subtle ways. We'll get back to that in a minute. Let's wrap this up.

I have a Susan B. Anthony dollar and a silver dollar for each of you. I want to challenge you to be a silver dollar, to live like a child of the King. People got annoyed with a dollar that looked too much like a quarter. Don't settle for being that kind of Christian. Don't try to see how close you can be to the world. You're living way below your value if you do.

So put these coins someplace where you'll see them. Let them be a reminder to you about how you're to be different in your heart first, and then let that affect what you say and do.

To reinforce this message, try using the term "Susan B." over the following days and weeks to describe any kind of a compromising thing for a Christian to say or do. For example, if you catch yourself complaining or arguing about something, say something like, "Well that was a real 'Susan B.' kind of thing for me to say. Sorry about that." If you do this a few times, the kids may pick it up. It'll be a reminder to you and your kids to avoid the danger of living like a "Susan B." Christian.

Laser Lesson

What's the Point?

Shed some light on the fact that it isn't enough for our friends to see Jesus in our lives. We need to tell them about Him too.

Things You'll Need

- Hand mirror
- Laser pointer (or flash-light)
- A darkened room

You can use a flashlight for this devotional, but if you can get your hands on a laser pointer it would be much better. (You can pick up a laser pointer for under $20. Better yet, ask around at church or at work. I'll bet you could borrow one.) The laser beam will reflect off the mirror more effectively—and let's face it, it's a whole lot more fun. You'll hold the attention of the kids longer that way.

Here We Go

We're going to learn a lesson with the help of a laser pointer today.

Pull out the laser pointer and direct the beam on different objects in the room. Point it on something dark, like maybe one of the kid's shirts.

Notice how the beam stays right where I'm aiming it? The light gets absorbed into whatever I point it at.

By this time the kids will want to try the laser themselves, I'll bet. They'll get their chance in a minute.

Now I want one of you to hold this hand mirror. We're going to see what happens when I direct the laser beam at it.

Direct the beam into the mirror and show them how it reflects to another spot or person in the room. Take your time with this; make it fun. Give each of them a chance to try it—but warn them not to aim it in anyone's eyes. Have them try the laser in the mirror to reflect the beam someplace else in the room. After they've had some fun with it, take the laser back and say something like this:

Just like a laser, God is light. If you're a Christian, He has directed His light on you. We can be "absorbers" or "reflectors." We absorb as we learn about God in church, Sunday school and so on. It's important to absorb, but it's not enough. If we're only "absorbers," people may see God's light in us, but that's about it. We need to be "reflectors" too.

Sure, people need to see God in us, but they also need us to bring the gospel directly to them. We've got to *tell* them. Here's what the Bible says about it:

> In the same way, let your light shine before men, that they may see your good deeds and praise your Father in heaven. (Matthew 5:16)

> But in your hearts set apart Christ as Lord. Always be prepared to give an answer to everyone who asks you to give the reason for the hope that you have. But do this with gentleness and respect. (1 Peter 3:15)

> That if you confess with your mouth, "Jesus is Lord," and believe in your heart that God raised him from the dead, you will be saved. (Romans 10:9)

Our friends need to see the light in us, and we need to share Him with them. How do we reflect His light?

Get some input from the kids, but don't let this drag out too long. By now you'll need to tell a story to keep their interest just a little longer so you can really drive the point home. Tell them something like this:

Imagine we're driving on a little country road in the middle of the night. It's pitch black and you're looking out the window at the stars. Suddenly something up ahead

Don't Blind Anyone!

Careful where you point that thing. You don't want to do "laser surgery" on anyone's eyes!

catches your eye. It's a farmhouse, and there are little flames licking out of an upstairs window.

"That farmhouse is on fire!" you shout, pointing ahead.

I pull the car over to the side of the road for a better look. We see a car in the driveway, so we know people are inside. While we watch, the flames get a little bigger as the fire spreads.

"We've got to warn them!" you tell me.

I'm not so convinced. "It's after midnight," I tell you. "The farmer and his family are probably asleep. He's not going to be too happy if we start pounding on his door to wake him up. Hey, he might even pull out a shotgun. The more I think about it, the more I think we better just keep going." I pull back onto the road and begin to accelerate.

"But we can't just leave them; they're gonna die!" you insist.

"It's really not our problem," I reply. "Maybe a neighbor will notice and give them a phone call. Yeah, that would be better. They'd know their neighbor and they'd probably trust them more."

"But what if a neighbor doesn't see the fire?" you whisper.

"Don't worry about that," I reply. "They probably have smoke detectors. They'll be OK." With that, I drive away, leaving the burning farmhouse behind us.

What would you think if I did something like that?

Tie It Together

Now it's time to get their reaction to your little story. Listen to what they say. You may be able to use it later. After they've given their opinion on how they feel about you just driving away from the burning farmhouse, they'll be ripe for you to bring the point home.

It would be crazy not to warn the farmer and his family. If they aren't warned, they'll die, right? You know, that's the way it is for your friends. It's like they're in a burning house. They're headed for hell, and they don't know how to be saved. Some don't even know they *need* to be saved. Like the farmer and his family, they're totally unaware of the danger that is headed their way.

Listen to this verse from the Bible.

> I have come into the world as a light, so that no one who believes in me should stay in darkness. (John 12:46)

That's why Jesus came. The Light of the World came here to rescue people. It's not good enough to just absorb His light. We need to *reflect* it. We need to bring the light to our friends, just like we reflected the laser beam off the mirror onto others.

Talk about how we can reflect that truth to others. You don't need my help on this. Let them brainstorm as long as they want. When the time is right . . . close in prayer.

Pie Face

What's the Point?

When their friends brag about doing wrong, do your kids know how God feels about that? You're going to show them—but first, a pie-eating contest!

Things You'll Need

- A pie big enough for each kid to have a large piece (pick a messy berry one if possible)
- (optional) Add a little ice cream or whipped cream on top
- A stopwatch
- A camera (you're going to want to remember this!)

Here We Go

You may want to start out with something like this:

We're going to give each of you a piece of pie to eat for devotions. Sound good?

Bring out the pie now. Give everyone a nice, big piece, but tell them to wait for the instructions.

There's just one little catch. You can't use a fork or spoon. You can't even use your hands. You're gonna have to bend over and put your face in it and eat it like an animal! Oh, and one more thing. I'm going to time you. The first one done with their entire piece wins. The plate must be completely clean.

The reason you want to time them is to keep them eating the pie fast. The faster they go, the messier they'll get. If you have more than one child, you could make it a race—maybe even award a prize for the winner. (Don't go crazy on the prize thing. Something simple is best, like offering to make the winner's bed for a week.) Be sure the camera is loaded and ready to go before you let them start eating.

Does everybody understand the rules? OK, let's go.

Start the stopwatch and snap a few pictures as they eat. Be sure to save a couple of shots for the end. When they are all done, take another picture of their messy faces and let them look at themselves in the mirror. They'll probably laugh at the sight of themselves with pie all over their faces. If that's the case, you're doing just fine. Don't let them wash it off until after devoes are done.

Well, that was great! What do you think about how your face looks?

Get some input. If the kids are older, they'll probably say it looks great. That's fine.

If you went to school with your face looking like that, how do you think you'd feel? Would you feel real proud and maybe even brag about it a little? "Hey guys, check out the cherries on my cheeks! Oh look—there's a cherry up my nose!" I don't think so. I'll bet you'd make sure your face was all cleaned up before you stepped out of the house.

Let me read a few verses to you (*emphasize the italicized part as you read*).

> For, as I have often told you before and now say again even with tears, many live as enemies of the cross of Christ. Their destiny is destruction, their god is their stomach, and *their glory is in their shame*. Their mind is on earthly things. But our citizenship is in heaven. And we eagerly await a Savior from there, the Lord Jesus Christ. (Philippians 3:18-20)

Tie It Together

Pie is a good thing, but it isn't supposed to be worn all over your face. If you went out in public with pie on you like that, you'd look

like an idiot. There's no way you'd go around bragging about what a mess you are.

That makes sense when it comes to pie, but what about other things? Some kids talk back to their parents, or swipe something from a store, and it doesn't seem to bother them. Sometimes they even brag about it to their friends. That's like walking around with pie on their faces.

That's what the verses we read are talking about. People tend to do wrong things and then brag about what they did. They "glory in their shame." You've seen it and heard it. They brag about what they did on a date or at a party, even though what they did was wrong. Some kids act like they're big stuff just because they drank some alcohol or smoked a cigarette.

Maybe they lied or cheated on a test and got away with it. They're actually proud of the fact. Maybe they were cruel to somebody by calling them names or picking on them. Instead of feeling bad about being cruel, it gives them a rush. In all these cases, and plenty more, they should feel ashamed about what they did, but instead they "glory" in it.

Even things that are good can be abused to our shame. Pie is good, but not when it's spread all over our face, right? How about sex? Sex is good, but not before marriage. Often teens will brag about what they've done sexually. Again, they glory in what should shame them. What do you think?

Stop and get some input from them. Can they give you an example of things they've heard kids brag about that were nothing to be proud of? It may be an eye-opener.

As Christians, we're to be different. Sure, we do the wrong thing sometimes, but we shouldn't be happy about that. It should bother us enough that we can't rest until we make the situation right. We're citizens of heaven. We're children of the King.

If you looked in the mirror right now, it would be pretty clear that you needed to wash your face. The Bible is like a mirror. When we read it, it helps us see what we're really like. Is there something that you need to get cleaned up? Something you need to make right? If so, take care of it. Let's stay in the Word and remember that we need to be different. We're children of the King. Let's live like it!

Remember those pictures you took? Get 'em processed, and have an extra copy made of each kid's "pie-face." Give it to them for a Bible bookmark or pop it in a little frame to put in their room somewhere. You could even put a copy of it on the fridge. In any case, jot down "Philippians 3:18-20" on the photo so they don't forget. It will be a good reminder for them about today's lesson—and for you too!

The Time and Place for Extra Space

What's the Point?

The more time you allow for Jesus in your life, the more benefit you'll get. We'll use a simple balancing act to make our point.

Things You'll Need

- Quarters—lots of 'em—at least a $10 roll
- A small cap from a pop or juice bottle

The lesson will be more powerful if you have a cap and quarters for each child listening. You may even let them pick a bottle of juice or pop to drink ahead of time. Tell them that they can drink it all, but they need to bring the cap to family devoes. That will make them a little curious.

Here We Go

Have the kids bring their pop or juice caps and tell them something like this:

We're going to play a little game today. I've got this roll of quarters here, and I want to see how many quarters you can stack up on that cap of yours.

Get a volunteer to start first. Have them hold the cap in one hand and stack quarters with the other. Let them stack as many quarters on top of the cap as they can. Keep count out loud as they stack them. When the stack falls, jot down the number of quarters they had just before the quarters fell. When everybody has had a turn, you might drop a little bombshell on them like this:

Oh, did I mention that you get to *keep* the number of quarters you were able to stack on the cap before they fell off?

Play it by ear here. If they want another chance, no big deal. It will work for the purposes of your illustration. After they are all done, quickly add up what they've "earned." Now you're ready to move on.

Well, you earned yourself a little money here. Just think how many quarters you would have had if I let you stack quarters on something bigger than a bottle cap. How would you like it if I let you keep the quarters you could pile up in a bowl, or maybe even a bucket?

Oh, yeah—their wheels are turning now! They're thinking how much money they could have gotten. Perfect. Maybe they're just a little upset that you only let them stack the quarters up on a little bitty cap. Even better. Now tell them something like this:

Yeah, can you imagine how much richer you would have been if you used a bowl or a bucket? A bucket has so much *space* (*key word here*) in it, it could easily hold hundreds of dollars in quarters. This little cap you were using doesn't have enough space to hold very many quarters. You'll never get rich using a cap. You need something bigger—something that has more space.

Let me read a verse to you. (*Put emphasis on the italicized part of the verse as you read.*)

> And she gave birth to her firstborn, a son. She wrapped him in cloths and placed him in a manger, because there was *no room for [him] in the inn*. (Luke 2:7)

Tie It Together

The innkeeper couldn't seem to find room for Jesus. There just wasn't enough space for Him. Who do you think lost out on that deal? The innkeeper! For 2,000 years the world has known him as the guy who couldn't make room for Jesus. He couldn't find a little space in the inn for the King of kings.

So what's that got to do with you, right? If it was *your* inn, you would have given Him the best room you had, don't you think? Sure you would—if you really knew it was Jesus.

Now let's forget about the little town of Bethlehem and the foolish innkeeper for a moment. Let's look at how much space *you* give to Jesus every day. You know, Jesus wants us to spend time with Him. How are you doing with finding Him room?

I know, I know—you have homework and school and TV and all kinds of things that take up space in your busy, important schedule. No room for Jesus? How different is that from the innkeeper?

Get some input from them. What do they think? Is it a fair comparison?

The thing of it is, the innkeeper blew it, but he didn't have a clue as to who he was leaving out in the cold that night. I wonder what he would have done if he knew the space would be for the Son of God. We don't have that excuse. We know who wants some space in our lives.

When we stacked up the quarters, the problem was space. The cap was too small for us to be able to pile a lot of quarters on it. Maybe you could buy a fast-food meal with it, but that would be about it. It's the same with giving God space in our life. If we get cheap and give Him just a capful, our benefit from it will be very limited, to put it mildly. If we give Him a bucket of time in our day, we'll have something that we can take to the bank. Of course, I'm not talking about money here, but about the world of benefit that we get from a closer walk with God.

I'll betcha that old innkeeper wishes he could go back and have another chance to find room for Jesus. How about you? Learn from the innkeeper—find some room for God. Here's what one of the writers of the psalms had to say about it:

> Oh, how I love your law! I meditate on it all day long. Your commands make me wiser than my enemies, for they are ever with me. I have more insight than all my teachers, for I meditate on your statutes. I have more understanding than the elders, for I obey your precepts. (Psalm 119:97-100)

Night Vision

What's the Point?

Use a darkened room to warn your kids about the danger of compromising their Christian standards.

Things You'll Need

This one is really easy to prepare for. All you need is a room in the house that will get nice and dark when you turn off the lights, but after a few minutes will allow you to see pretty decently as your eyes become accustomed to it. You'll also want to have a couple of pieces of paper and a pencil or pen for each person.

Here We Go

Get the kids together in the room you have picked out. Be sure the lights in the room are super bright to begin with. Here's the drill: Give each child a piece of paper and something to write with. Tell the kids that you're going to turn out the lights, and as soon as you do, they need to quickly write their name, address, phone number and something else—maybe the name of their favorite car or truck.

Speed is critical here. You want them to write it all down before their eyes begin to adjust to the light. I'd give them about twenty seconds, max. Ideally you'll get some extremely sloppy writing by doing it that way. When the time is up, collect the papers, but don't turn on the lights.

When your eyes adjust to the dark enough to see clearly, have the kids write their name, address, phone number and their favorite car or truck again, on a different piece of paper. This time, the writing should be much neater.

Flip on the lights and watch everybody wince a little. When their eyes have readjusted, compare each person's papers. Look at the difference with the one written immediately after the lights went out as compared to the one written a few minutes later. Have fun teasing them a little on how sloppy the one paper is. Then ask them something like this:

OK, you wrote two papers in the same room, with the same lighting, and both within minutes of each other. One reminds me of the way you wrote when you were just a little kid, and the other doesn't look too bad. Why was your writing so different on these two?

The answer is obvious, but let them speak up anyway. You're looking for them to say they couldn't see well enough the first time because their eyes hadn't adjusted to the dark yet. Bingo. This is going great. Let's move on.

Yeah, at first we couldn't see a thing. After a few minutes, our eyes began to adjust to the dark. Writing wasn't so difficult anymore. It's like that when we go out at night too. When we step out of a lighted room into the dark outside, we have to be really careful as we walk. After a couple of minutes we can see pretty well just by the light of the moon.

That can happen to us as Christians too. Let me read you a few verses.

> How can a young man keep his way pure? By living according to your word. (Psalm 119:9)

> Turn my eyes away from worthless things; preserve my life according to your word. (119:37)

> Your word is a lamp to my feet and a light for my path. (119:105)

> So let us put aside the deeds of darkness and put on the armor of light. (Romans 13:12)

Some Man-to-Man Advice

This devotional sounds really easy, and it is, but you have to test it first. I know, I know. Men hate to bother testing something we're sure will work just fine. Check it out anyway, just to be sure. If the room is so dark that your eyes won't adjust well enough to write, you won't be able to get the point across clearly.

For you were once darkness, but now you are light in the Lord. Live as children of light (for the fruit of the light consists in all goodness, righteousness and truth) and find out what pleases the Lord. Have nothing to do with the fruitless deeds of darkness, but rather expose them. (Ephesians 5:8-11)

Tie It Together

As Christians, we're supposed to walk in the light. We're supposed to live the way God has outlined in the Bible. Now, we don't always do that, right? Sometimes we don't walk in the light, but we walk in the ways of this world instead. What do I mean by that?

Get their thoughts here. This could be a good chance to learn about them. Take whatever they give you and build on it to make your point.

Yeah, we start living like the world. Instead of seeking God's direction, we make decisions without considering Him. Instead of relying on God's power, we just do things with our own steam. Instead of guarding our minds from wrong thoughts, we let our minds drift.

Instead of being considerate of others, we live selfishly. Instead of serving others, we want to be served. Instead of being humble, we are proud. Instead of running from evil, we toy with it. Instead of being thankful, we find reasons to complain.

That's called walking in darkness, and after a while, you get kind of used to it. You know you're a Christian, and you may think you're living like one. Chances are, though, you aren't walking entirely in the light. How do we know if we're walking in semidarkness?

See what they say. They may be "in the dark" on this one. That's typical. Let's bring this devotional in for a landing.

How about the Bible? Yeah, the Bible is our light, and when we read it, we often see how we're compromising with the darkness in some way.

Remember how bright the lights looked when we turned them back on? That's how it is with the Bible. I might be reading a passage that I haven't read in a long time, and wham! It's like someone just turned on the lights. The Bible is really clear about some issues—in fact it's a lot more clear than I had remembered. I had been drifting into the shadows, and didn't realize it until I'd really seen the light of God's Word. The Bible often shows us how we're compromising as Christians.

Can you give me some examples of how Christians live in darkness and seem to adjust to it as if it were normal or OK for a Christian to live that way?

We're trying to get them to think. See what they say. Hopefully they'll get beyond obvious things like "drugs" or things like that. You may prompt them with more subtle things like pride, selfishness, arguing and complaining. It's what they read, watch on TV, and think about. All of these are examples of darkness that can creep into our lives.

We can get pretty used to living in the shadows in a lot of ways. We can feel pretty comfortable living in the dark. It happens to plenty of Christians. They adjust to being in the dark, just like you were able to write clearly in the dark after a while.

It's not where we belong, though. As you read your Bible, ask God to show you where you're compromising, where you're living in the dark. Ask Him to help you stay in the light. Ask Him to help you be a light in a world of darkness.

That's Not Fair

What's the Point?

You'll use the game of Monopoly to teach your kids a very important lesson: Life isn't fair.

Things You'll Need

This one is easy. All you need is a game of Monopoly. If you don't have one, just borrow one from a friend. This classic family game is probably on the closet shelf of almost anyone you know. You'll also need some nerves of steel. You're going to change the game rules a bit, and you can't back down and get soft when one of the kids is in a bad spot.

Here We Go

All right, here's how we're going to do this. We want to put the kids in situations where they feel you're not being fair with them. Now, we don't want to go overboard here, but the more frustrated we can get them (within bounds of reason), the better.

So, announce to the kids that you're going to play Monopoly for devotions. That ought to bring a couple of strange looks. Proceed to explain that you're going to play by a little different set of rules than they may be used to.

The new rules are simple. You make 'em. Yeah, the deal is that you may be making up some new rules as you go along. You'll also be the banker. The more people playing, the better. If you only have one child in devotions, maybe he can invite a friend. You'd like to get at least three or four players.

Hopefully you'll end up playing too, or your spouse. That's fine. If your spouse is playing, be sure she knows what you're up to. In fact, she can help by saying, "That's not fair!" during the game once in a while.

Sit the kids down and start handing out the money. Here's your first chance to be unfair. Give a stack of $100s to one person, a stack of $20s to another. Give one a stack of $500s, and a handful of $1s and $5s to another. Are you getting the picture? You are creating classes of people. You've made some wealthy, some middle class and some very poor players here.

Ask them to count their money and give you the total. You might already be getting some protests from the less wealthy players. Dismiss their complaints by saying you just want to start the game and that maybe you'll take care of some of those petty details later.

Next, grab the properties and hand some of those out. You might take a handful and ask one player to pick the five they want. Then ask another player to pick two. Invite another player to pick three, but with their eyes closed. See how unfair you can be? This should start to drive the kids nuts. All this time you have to be very casual about it like it doesn't affect you.

Before you even start playing, announce a hotel sale. Make a one-time offer. Five hotels for $500. Of course, some players don't have enough money for this. Ah, the poor get poorer and the rich get richer. Have you heard anyone howl that this isn't fair yet? If so, you're right on track. If not, your kids are being way too polite.

So, start playing the game. You don't want the game to go long. The ones without money will be frustrated and won't be having too much fun, so you'll have to keep it moving. Feel free to change any rules you need to as you go along. Don't be consistent. That would be fair. Make the rules change. If someone rolls doubles they expect two turns. That's fine. Now, when someone else rolls doubles, make them lose a turn. When someone passes go, go ahead and give them their $200. Give the next person $20.

Here are some other ideas to make the game unfair. Make the railroads a poison property. If someone lands there, he goes to jail, or he's out of the game, or he gives all his property to the player to his right. When someone lands on a property, allow the property owner to put a hotel on it right then so he can collect more money for it. Be sure each person gets a taste of your unfairness during the course of the game.

I'd imagine some players are miserable by this time. You'll have to keep the game pretty short. Maybe some are already out of the game. That's OK. Now stop the game and talk about it before you go too long and lose them. You might say something like this:

OK, how many of you enjoyed playing Monopoly like this?

I would expect most of them didn't like it at all (except maybe the one you gave the stack of $500 bills to!).

What didn't you like about playing this way?

Hopefully they'll complain about the game not being fair. Perfect. You've done your job. Now let's make some sense of this.

Tie It Together

OK, if I'm hearing you right, you found the game to be frustrating because you didn't think I was being fair, right? I mean, I gave some a lot of money to start with, and others got a lot less. Some got to pick good proper-ties, while others had to pick blindly. I wasn't playing fair at all.

We all seem to want to see things done fairly, not just in a game like this, but in life. Time has taught me that life isn't always fair. Some people seem to have it easy. They have the looks, the friends, the money, the talent. Others don't seem to catch a break. Jerks get away with doing bad things. Nice kids get hurt. Some kids have both parents in the home, others only have one parent on the scene. A drunk driver kills an innocent child, or a mom, or a dad. He destroys some other family, and he doesn't even get hurt or go to jail.

The truth is, there seem to be a lot more ex-amples of things around us that *aren't* fair than the other way around. This is nothing new. The Bible is chock-full of examples of people who got a raw deal. Can you name me any?

All right, give them a chance to think and give some input. If they need some help, be prepared to throw out some names. Give them a couple, then see if they can think of others.

Noah—honors God in a perverted society and is ridiculed for it

Joseph—sold into slavery because his brothers were jealous of him

Moses—tries to help a slave and becomes a fugitive

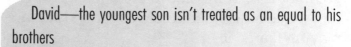

David—the youngest son isn't treated as an equal to his brothers

Stephen—stoned to death for speaking the truth about Jesus

Paul—imprisoned and beaten for preaching the gospel

The Bible is full of examples. When you think they've named enough to get them to realize that the "life isn't fair" issue isn't something new, go ahead and move on.

See, life isn't fair. That's the way it's been ever since Adam and Eve sinned. Now, sometimes things work out for a person eventually. Sure, they get a raw deal, but later they get treated right.

Noah—survived the flood, his skeptics drowned

Joseph—became a ruler in Egypt and his brothers needed his help

Moses—came back to rescue and lead his people

David—became king

Other times, an unfair situation never gets "paid back":

Stephen—died as they stoned him unfairly

Paul—was constantly persecuted for his faith

Stephen and Paul had plenty of company. Listen to these verses about other Christians.

Others were tortured and refused to be released, so that they might gain a better resurrection. Some faced jeers and flogging, while still others were chained and put in prison. They were stoned; they were sawed in two; they were put to death by the sword. They went about in sheepskins and goatskins, destitute, persecuted and mistreated—the world was not worthy of them. (Hebrews 11:35-38)

We'd like to see everything fair in life. People who do good things should have good things happen to them. They should live to a ripe old age and be free from worry, pain and trouble. People who do bad things should pay the consequences. This rarely seems to be the case. Life just isn't fair.

Now, if I left it there, this would be a pretty dismal thought. But there's something we need to remember: *God* is fair. God is just. God always does the right thing. He doesn't always do things on our schedule, though. See, God will reward the good, and He'll punish the bad, but *He* picks the timing to do it.

Sometimes He rewards and punishes here on earth in our lifetimes. Most of the time He reserves judgment and administering justice until after a person's life is over. Does this make sense to you?

Hey, this is a tough subject. You want to be sure they're tracking with you before you wrap it up. So get some input. Maybe all you'll get is a head nod. That's OK, as long as they're grasping the concept.

Let me read you a couple more verses.

The eyes of the LORD are everywhere, keeping watch on the wicked and the good. (Proverbs 15:3)

For he has set a day when he will judge the world with justice by the man he has appointed. (Acts 17:31)

Just as man is destined to die once, and after that to face judgment, so Christ was sacrificed once to take away the sins of many people. (Hebrews 9:27-28)

We could sum it up like this: God sees everything that goes on. He's keeping score, and someday there will be a payday just as sure as the sun comes up in the morning. Sure, it's frustrating to see bad people prosper and good people get hurt. God will settle the score, though.

That's something we all need to remember, especially when we think something isn't fair. We don't have to get all bent out of shape when we think somebody is unfair and getting away with it. God will take care of it, even if it's when that person stands before God to be judged when his life on earth is over.

OK, we gotta quit or we'll lose 'em for sure. You've driven home the point; they get the picture. You may want to end it with something like this:

You know, we've all blown it, and we all deserve judgment. Thank God for the forgiveness He's offered through Jesus. We've been unfair to others at times. Others have been unfair to us. Let's ask God to forgive us for the things we've been unfair about, and trust Him to deal with the ones who have treated us unfairly, OK?

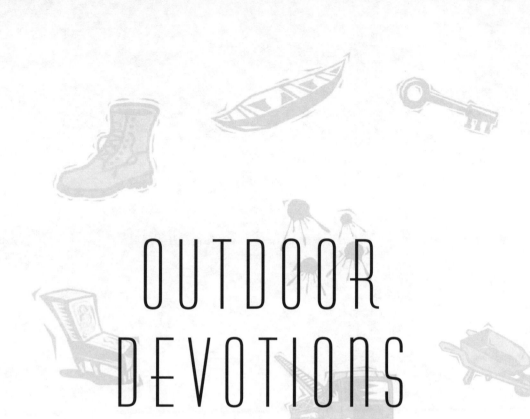

OUTDOOR

DEVOTIONS

Mashed Potatoes

What's the Point?

You and the kids will have a lot of fun throwing mashed potatoes and eggs, and watching them explode on a plywood target. Then you'll talk about a type of "explosion" that isn't so much fun: exploding in anger.

Things You'll Need

- Big batch of mashed potatoes
- At least 6 eggs for each kid to throw (including yourself)
- Plywood to use as a backboard

You can be a little creative with this one. Use a sheet of plywood to use as a backboard to throw the eggs and mashed potatoes against. Yes, I said throw. Draw a big bull's-eye on the plywood. This is beginning to sound fun already, eh? (The plywood won't go to waste. You'll need it for two other devotionals in this book.)

In case you have any doubts, yes, you must do this one outside.

Eggs and potatoes are cheap, so don't skimp. They're going to love throwing this stuff, so get plenty of it.

Here We Go

Find a good spot outside to set up your plywood target. Get the eggs and mashed potatoes, then call the kids together. You might expect some weird looks when they see the eggs and potatoes. You might start out with something like this:

I think you're going to like this. I have all these eggs and this giant bowl of mashed potatoes. I'm thinking you'll get a kick out of throwing the eggs and potatoes at the target just to see them explode. Sound like fun?

Of course it sounds like fun! Admit it—you're itching to throw, aren't you? Imagine how the kids feel! But you need to control the chaos here. Let the kids step up to the line one at a time and wing an egg or a handful of mashed potatoes at the board.

You're the cheerleader. "Wow, great shot!" and other exclamations of approval should be flowing from your mouth as often as they're pitching the potatoes and eggs. Laugh, have fun. I don't think I need to tell you to take a turn yourself. (Maybe I need to remind you to let the kids have a turn!)

Continue to let the kids take turns until you run out of ammo or the police stop by. You'll want the kids to wash the taters off their hands, but wait to hose down the backboard and clean up that mess until after devoes are done. You might start off with something like this:

Now *that* was fun. Just seeing those eggs and potatoes *explode* on the backboard was a riot. What do you think?

Let them express how much fun they had with it too. Now we're going to make some sense of this whole thing.

Eggs and potatoes exploding is fun. Destructive, messy, but definitely fun. There's another kind of explosion that is often destructive and can get pretty messy, but it definitely *isn't* fun. Anyone care to venture a guess as to what I'm driving at?

Let them take a guess or two, then keep rolling. They probably won't get the answer yet; we're just trying to get the wheels rolling in their heads.

I'm talking about anger. Yeah, exploding in anger—destructive, messy, not fun. Let me read you a couple of verses.

> A wise man fears the LORD and shuns evil, but a fool is hotheaded and reckless. A quick-tempered man does foolish things. (Proverbs 14:16-17)

> A patient man has great understanding, but a quick-tempered man displays folly. (14:29)

> A hot-tempered man stirs up dissension, but a patient man calms a quarrel. (15:18)

> A fool gives full vent to his anger, but a wise man keeps himself under control. (29:11)

An angry man stirs up dissension, and
a hot-tempered one commits many sins.
(Proverbs 29:22)

Whoa—talk about some heavy-duty verses
condemning a quick, explosive temper! What
do these verses tell you?

They don't have the verses in front of them, so this could be
hard for them. See what they say, then go on and recap.

Tie It Together

That's right—hot-headed, quick-tempered
people are going to commit a lot of sin.
They're going to make their own situations
worse. They're going to stir up dissension, or
stir up more trouble for themselves. They're
going to do foolish, stupid things. Not a
pretty picture, is it?

If I said, "Raise your hand if you'd like to
make trouble for yourself, commit a lot of sin,
make a lot of mistakes and do some really stupid things," how many of you would be raising your hands?

If you have teenagers, I would expect you'll see somebody
raise his hand. That's OK, they're having fun. They like to tease
when it comes to stuff like this.

God's Word tells us that a quick temper is
a very bad thing. When we get upset fast,
we're really harming ourselves. We're also
disobeying God and fighting against His
plans. Listen to this verse:

My dear brothers, take note of this: Everyone should be quick to listen, slow to speak and slow to become angry, for man's anger does not bring about the righteous life that God desires. (James 1:19-20)

We're commanded to be slow to anger. When we explode in anger, we're going against God. Now that *is* stupid, isn't it? Anger generally stems from pride, and God hates that. We'll save that issue for another devotional. There's a great verse in Proverbs you gotta hear:

Like a city whose walls are broken down is a man who lacks self-control. (Proverbs 25:28)

In Bible times, a broken wall around a city was serious stuff. A wall around a city was its protection from armies and raiders that would steal and kill. If we don't control our anger, we're unprotected and living in a dangerous situation, just like a city without walls. The Bible tells us we are opening ourselves up for a lot of hurt.

Would you work on that? Self-control is something God will give you if you ask. Ask Him to help you control your temper. It's for your own good.

Oh, one more thing. Anger usually makes a mess of things, just like the mashed potatoes and eggs against the plywood. Cleaning up the plywood isn't fun, but the messes explosive anger leaves behind are much worse. Keep that in mind as you help me clean up.

Important lesson, even for dads, isn't it? They got the message, so let's not beat this issue to death. If a short fuse is a problem you wrestle with, you have to work on it. You're the example to the kids, and that's the lesson they'll really *remember*.

We all blow it at times. If you do, ask the Lord and the family to forgive you. Ask God to help you with the self-control aspect. It's part of the fruit of the Spirit, and it would certainly be God's will for you. Let's work on it, OK?

Paddle Battle

What's the Point?

Paddling a canoe without real paddles is a reminder of how ineffective life can be without prayer.

Things You'll Need

Ideally, you'll need a canoe and paddles to go with it. Where are you going to find this? Ask around at church. You'll find a connection somewhere. If you're near water or a camp, there's probably a good chance someone will let you borrow or rent one.

You'll also need a couple of alternative paddles, too. Here are some suggestions: ping-pong paddles; tennis or racketball rackets; baseball bats; or maybe the kids can use only their hands as paddles. Anything will get the point across.

You may want to plan a picnic lunch or at least a snack to break out after the canoe activity is over. After all, paddling works up an appetite.

One last thought. Have the kids wear swimsuits or bring a change of clothes along. Kids can't be around water and stay dry.

Here We Go

OK, grab the kids and go to the lake or stream where you'll have your devoes. I know you're anxious to get in that canoe, but be sure to have life jackets all around and follow basic water safety rules.

Pick a point for the kids to race to and back while paddling the canoe. You're going to time them. Now, if it's just you and one child, you'll be in the canoe paddling too.

Even better, have your child invite some friends. If you have enough kids to set up a little competition for a race, that would make things more exciting. Have some fun with this.

Spread out your assortment of nonconventional "paddles" and say something like this to the kids.

All right, guys. We're going to have a little canoe race here. We're going to time you paddling from here to [*some designated point*]. Here's the trick. You'll pick from one of the paddles I have here for your first heat. I'll record your time. Then I'm going to let you do it again with regular canoe paddles. We'll compare the two times.

Now, if you have enough kids to make two teams, I'd throw a little incentive in there. Here are two ideas. You could make the losing team get back in the canoe and the rest of the kids get to tip them over. You could also offer the winning team the first pick of the pop and snacks you brought in the cooler.

Let the race begin. You record the time as they struggle to make progress with their makeshift paddles. Then record the time with the real paddles. If you have more than one team, you may want to hold off on announcing the winners until after you've tied this together in the devotional part. That will extend the fun and anticipation.

When all the racing is done and you've recorded the times, tell the kids to sit down for a few minutes while you make some sense of this event. You might say something like this:

It was pretty obvious that using those goofy paddles instead of regular ones was going to slow you down. If you had to go a long distance or were in a real race, you'd want to pick which paddles?

OK, expect some wise-guy answers here. We're just warming them up. They know the right answer, whether they give it to you or not. They're probably still having too much fun to settle down and get serious. That's fine.

Well, if you had to go a long way, or you wanted to get someplace quick, most people would pick the regular canoe paddles. If we were in rough water or a stream with a current, you wouldn't have a chance using a ping-pong paddle.

This is like life in some respects. It's like we're traveling through life in a canoe. God gives us the choice of paddles. Just like a ca-

noe paddle, there is one type of paddle He's designed for us to use so that we can maximize our effectiveness in life. It's prayer. Yeah, life is way too tough for us not to rely on God through prayer.

Let me read a few verses to you.

> Trust in the LORD with all your heart and lean not on your own understanding; in all your ways acknowledge him, and he will make your paths straight. (Proverbs 3:5-6)

> Be joyful always; pray continually; give thanks in all circumstances, for this is God's will for you in Christ Jesus. (1 Thessalonians 5:16-18)

> The prayer of a righteous man is powerful and effective. (James 5:16)

Tie It Together

Now, God gives us the choice of paddles. Instead of prayer, we may pick something else to get us through life. Got any ideas what I might mean here?

Get some input to see if they're tracking with you yet. If not, don't worry. They will as you give some examples.

Oftentimes prayer is the last thing we choose. We try to go it on our own first. We choose to use our own creativity, our own smarts. We take the advice of friends before we pray and ask God to lead us. We rely on our own strength, our own abilities, even luck

to get through tough times we may face. Some people rely on money or depend on others. Most kids rely solely on their moms or dads.

If prayer is like a canoe paddle, if it's the tool God's designed for the job, then we know it's the most effective way to get through life too.

It's pretty easy to get impatient and just grab one of the other "paddles" available to us. That's the battle of the paddles. Prayer is the most effective over the long haul, but it's not the easiest one to pick up. It's rarely our first choice. But the fact is, prayer is absolutely necessary if we want to get hooked into God's power.

The Bible is full of examples of how effective prayer can be. God wants us to talk to Him daily—not just before meals, but throughout the day. Ask Him to guide you, to give you strength to do what you should do. What else can you be talking to Him about?

This is a key input time. Get them thinking. See what kind of ideas you get from them. When the time is right, sum it up with their feedback and your thoughts.

Guys, life is tough. If we want to go where God intends, if we want to become the people He has planned, we can't make it on our own power, abilities, talents or smarts. We need

His power. We need to pray. We need to be willing to do it His way, the way He designed.

Would you work on that? Make prayer, talking to God, as much a part of your life as eating and sleeping.

Now, let me share the canoe race times with you and tell you who the winner is. Then I think there may be a little penalty for the loser (*if you were planning the little dunk in the water*) and first choice of the snacks for the winner!

Nice job. They won't forget this, but they may forget to pray. It's tough to do. It's a good chance for you to model this necessary discipline in everyday life. Share with them about things you're praying about, things you'd like them to pray for you on and answers to prayer. Ask them things you can pray for them about—you know, the daily kind of stuff. Help them see the naturally important part prayer has in your day.

No Sweat

What's the Point?

Giving the kids a job to do, while providing an easy opportunity to avoid it, sets things up perfectly for a talk about laziness.

Things You'll Need

You'll need to have a couple of jobs in your head that you'd like the kids to do. Hey, this sounds good already, doesn't it? You'll also need a couple of bucks to run out for some ice cream as a reward.

Here We Go

Have you figured out a job you'd like the kids to do? For me, it was washing the car. That may not work if you're doing this in the winter. In that case, pick some indoor job you'd like done like vacuuming, washing floors or anything else the kids could do without your direct supervision. (By the way, there's no reason to choose a job that is overly hard or unpleasant to do; don't push your luck!) For the sake of simplicity, I'll refer to "washing the car" in the following pages.

You'll need to figure out what you're going to do for a reward too. I made it "going out for ice cream" in the following pages, but you could make it pizza or anything else that the kids would really enjoy.

Get the kids together and say something like this:

Who'd like to go out with me for a little ice cream?

I'd expect everyone would be willing to go. Now it's time to tell them about the little "catch" to getting the reward.

Oh, there is one thing I'd like you to get done. Would you guys help me out by washing the car first?

Let's see how they react. I'll guess you'll hear a little moaning and groaning about having to do some work. Perfect. Let's put the bait out in front of them.

What? Would you rather get the ice cream *before* you wash the car?

OK. Here's the tricky part. Ideally, for the sake of the devotional, the kids will choose to get the ice cream first. That will make teaching this lesson easier. Now, if they say "Let's get the work done first," don't panic. I'm sure there's a logical explanation for their bizarre behavior.

Seriously, if your kids react that way, thank God for such great kids and get to work. You can still teach the devotional from the viewpoint that many kids would have chosen ice cream first.

Anyway, if (when) they *do* express an interest in going for ice cream first, you might say something like this:

So let me get this straight. You want the ice cream first, and you'll wash the car on your own right away when we get back?

They should heartily agree at this point. Shrug and go along with it.

OK, let's go.

Go out for ice cream, but don't mention washing the car again. OK, I admit it, we're trying to lead the kids into a trap here. Enjoy the ice cream. Take your time. When you get back home again, find some excuse to keep you away from them for awhile. Make a phone call, whatever.

Make yourself scarce for a bit. You're stalling to see if they wash the car as per your little agreement. After about thirty minutes, get the kids together. If they *did* wash the car on their own, praise them for it. Go ahead and share the devotional, just change it as necessary. Explain that many kids would have been lazy and not washed the car without being nagged to do it. You're proud they didn't do it that way, and that laziness is something we must fight in ourselves. Just go on with the devotional from there.

Enough with the wishful thinking. I'm going to guess your kids get busy with other things when you get home from the ice cream. I'd guess that they won't get around to washing the car. After you've given them thirty minutes or so, call them together and say something like this:

I'm all set with the stuff I had to do. How did the car washing go?

Ah-ha. Guilty looks? Excuses? They were going to do it later? Blah, blah, blah. Kids can get pretty creative, can't they? OK, let's take charge here.

Hmmm. Let me read you a couple of verses.

All hard work brings a profit, but mere talk leads only to poverty. (Proverbs 14:23)

"If a man will not work, he shall not" eat. (2 Thessalonians 3:10)

Tie It Together

Well, you can say you forgot, that you were going to do it later, or whatever.

When you're told to do something, or when you agree to do something and you stall it off, we call it laziness.

You may get some protests on this. Nobody likes to be called lazy. Wave off their excuses. You have the floor. Keep going.

The Bible tells us that laziness is bad stuff. That one verse says that if a person doesn't work, he shouldn't eat.

This is a lot like life. People often want the rewards first, and they'll promise to do the work later. They want a raise at work. "Give me this raise and I'll show you what I can do." Rewards first, work later. People get themselves in credit card debt that way too. "I'll just charge this and pay for it with my next paycheck." Rewards first, work later.

That isn't how God operates. Work first, rewards later. That's His plan. He doesn't even promise you'll get the rewards right away. His best rewards will be reserved for us in heaven.

Just like washing the car. That was the work. Getting the ice cream was the reward. Given a choice, most kids would choose to get the rewards up front. Sometimes the work just never gets done that way.

"Rewards first and work later" is how most people like it. Better yet, "rewards now and skip the work if you can." That's the world's

way, not God's. He doesn't want us to fall into a lazy pattern like that, and I don't either. Make sense?

You're looking for a little input here. I think they'll get the message. They may not do anything more than nod, but that's OK. Let's not keep beating the same drum here. Wrap it up.

Well that's it. Will you work on fighting the natural tendency of being lazy?

I expect you'll get some kind of positive feedback from them, if only a grunt. Good enough. One last item of unfinished business. Trust me, they're still hoping to get out of washing the car.

Oh, one last thing. (*Smile*) Wash the car now.

Peter, Paul and Paint Balls

What's the Point?

Forgiving each other may not sound like a fun topic—until we pull out the paint ball gun, that is!

Things You'll Need

- A paint ball gun and a bunch of paint balls (Talk to some dads you know. One of them is bound to have a gun you can borrow. You may even decide to bite the bullet and buy one. You can get them pretty cheap at a department store.)
- A sheet of plywood, at least 4' x 4'. This will be the target you'll be shooting at. (Optionally, you could paint the plywood white on one side, so the paint ball splatters show up a little better. As long as you're at it, paint a nice big bull's-eye in the middle.)
- Some cheap latex paint and a brush or roller (you'll be using the paint to cover over the splatters on the plywood, so it has to be very close to the color of the paint balls you buy)

Here We Go

Let's get one thing straight right now: The kids will be just as eager to fire that baby as you are, but be sure to take a minute to cover some safety rules, such as not aiming the gun at anything but the plywood target, staying out of the line of fire, etc. Let's not have any accidents, OK? (I can see the headline now: "Parent Shoots Child with Paint Ball Gun to Teach Kids about Love." People just won't understand.)

If some of your kids are older, get one of them to help you out. Show him the gun ahead of time. Have him help you set things up and keep an eye out for safety concerns. When you're all ready, call the kids together and say something like this:

We're going to have some *fun* today, guys. I have a paint ball gun here and a target I'd like us to hit. Is anyone interested in trying this?

They're just as anxious to shoot as you are. My advice? Take the first shot yourself. It's a good chance to show them how to work it—and it may be the only chance you'll get to shoot!

Let each of the kids take some shots. If they're enjoying it, take your time. Remember, it's the devotional time you need to keep short, not the fun. It will only reinforce the point of the devotional in their memory.

When you're ready to move on, get the paint ball gun back in your hands and say something like this:

Now *that* was fun, huh? Take a look at that target. Pretty good shootin', I'd say.

You're probably wondering where I'm going with this devotional, right? Take a look at our target over there. Think of it as representing your life. And the paint ball splatters? That's the sin in our life.

We all sin. Sometimes it's fun to sin—why else would we do it so much? We enjoy it at the time. Sometimes we sin without thinking—we don't even notice that we've done something wrong. Like when we say something that hurts someone.

One thing that sin and paint balls have in common is that they both leave a mess. How can sin make a mess of things?

Listen carefully to what they say here; you may get some interesting feedback. Don't hang on this long, however. We have too much ground to cover.

Our relationships with others are one of the biggest things that can get messed up by sin. When you sin by being selfish, proud or careless in what you say or do, you hurt others. That happens right here in our own family. Each of you has been affected at times when another member of the family sins. That's the type of sin we'll zero in on right now.

Let me share some verses with you:

Above all, love each other deeply, because love covers over a multitude of sins. (1 Peter 4:8)

You'll be happy to know your investment will be used again in another devotional in this book entitled "Paint Balls and Prayer." (Whoa—what a holy-sounding title! Maybe you should buy one of those paint ball guns. We'll use the same piece of plywood too. Now we really are getting thrifty, huh?)

If Great Aunt Matilda Is Visiting . . .

If you're concerned about the kids using a "gun," here's an alternative: Pick up the paint balls from the store, but forget the gun. Lay the plywood down flat on the ground and have a hammer handy. During the part of the devotional that calls for the kids to fire the gun, instead have the kids splatter the paint balls on the plywood with the hammer. It may be a little messier, but they'll still enjoy it. It

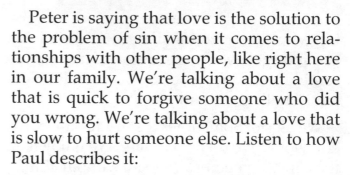

would probably be good to have them wear some safety goggles as well, just to avoid paint in the eyes.

Peter is saying that love is the solution to the problem of sin when it comes to relationships with other people, like right here in our family. We're talking about a love that is quick to forgive someone who did you wrong. We're talking about a love that is slow to hurt someone else. Listen to how Paul describes it:

> Love is patient, love is kind. It does not envy, it does not boast, it is not proud. It is not rude, it is not self-seeking, it is not easily angered, it keeps no record of wrongs. (1 Corinthians 13:4-5)

Tie It Together

When you feel you've been wronged by someone else in the family, you have a choice to make. The choice has to do with how you're going to react to the wrong.

Sometimes we just sort of tuck those hurts away in our memory, and then later—maybe when we're arguing about something else—we remind the person of all the things they've done to us. That's called keeping a record of wrongs. According to God's description of love, we can't do that.

Sometimes we get upset with the person who wronged us and we let them know it—we fly off the handle and give them a piece of our minds. That's being easily angered. That isn't love either.

Sometimes we just get totally offended by what the person did. The *nerve* of them to do that to you! That's an example of being proud.

All three of these reactions to someone who sins against us are wrong. They are not examples of responding in love. If we don't respond in love, we're not obeying what Paul tells us we should do in First Corinthians 13. If we're not obeying the Bible, that means that *we're* sinning. *We're* doing wrong by keeping a record, by getting upset or by being proud. We're not obeying God by reacting in love. What do you think about that?

Give them a chance to process this. If they give you some feedback, hey, that's great. Don't worry if they don't. Believe me, they're tracking with you. Let's make sure they have it.

Now honestly, when you are treated badly by someone, especially here in our own family, you feel justified to get upset, or to be offended, or to keep that offense on some kind of list in your memory, right?

You're looking for a nod or some kind of positive response here. Whether or not they give it to you, you have to move on.

Well, God's Word tells us otherwise. I need a little help here.

Pull out the paint that matches the paint balls. Hand out a brush or two and have them help you paint the entire side of the plywood. When it's totally covered, wrap it up.

Pretty tough to see the paint ball stains now, huh? We've covered them all up. That's what God wants us to do when someone sins against us. He wants us to react in love. We don't get all upset. We don't get frustrated and keep a list of what they did wrong to us. We don't get all proud and offended. No, we love them. We forgive their wrongs toward us. Peter tells us that love covers a multitude of sins. How can we do this?

Pretty key question. Give them a chance to think, then close it up.

I guess it would help for us to remember that God loves us and forgives us when we sin. We're supposed to forgive others in the same way. When we do, it's like we paint over the whole mess. We don't just bury it. The sin isn't hidden—it's gone. We remember to love that person who wronged us. It's tough to do, and we need God's help. Does it sound like a good thing to work on?

Hey, if you get a nod, consider your mission accomplished.

This is a pretty important thing—a big key to great relationships with family and friends for your whole life. That was the advice that Paul and Peter would give you if they were here with you today. Here's one last tip from Paul on the subject.

In your anger do not sin: Do not let the sun go down while you are still angry, and do not give the devil a foothold. (Ephesians 4:26-27)

Here's what he's saying: Sure, when somebody wrongs you in some way, it's easy to get ticked about it. You don't want that to make *you* guilty of sinning, though. Remember how you need to react in love. Take care of the situation right away. Don't wait until tomorrow. Forgive the person, and paint away their sin against you by remembering God's love for you and how we're to love others too. OK?

OK, you're all set. Remember to hang onto the plywood. You can use it for the devotional entitled "Paint Balls and Prayer." You'll even have it painted the same color as your paint balls, which is exactly the way that devotional starts. Keep the paint ball gun in a safe place. Let's not tempt the kids to try this when you're not around!

Beauty Is a Beast

What's the Point?

A trip to a used car lot will illustrate the importance of picking a date (or a mate) based on what's inside, not just on looks.

Things You'll Need

This one is easy. You're going to take the kids to a used car lot, so you'll want to scope out a place in advance. Personally, I'd rather clean toilets than venture onto a used car lot. The kids will enjoy it though, especially the boys.

Now, you'll probably want to find a used car lot that's on the smaller side—nothing too massive. Here's why: You're going to ask the kids to look around and pick their dream used car if money was no object—but if you pick a lot that's too big, you'll have a harder time getting them to make a decision. It would be especially nice if you found a lot that had all the cheesy slogans on the used car windshields—"A Real Honey," "Like New," "Low Miles," "No Rust"—you get the idea.

Here We Go

I gotta tell you, this is a key lesson. The kind of person you date could be the kind you make your mate. How many times did you hear that when you were dating? Now it's your turn to preach it. Remember, marriage is for keeps—if you get a "lemon," you can't trade it in for a different model!

Anyway, get the kids together and say something like this:

All right, guys—pile in the car. We're going to have a little fun.

I wouldn't bother explaining where you're going until you're almost there. You might say something like this:

We're going to a used car lot, and here's what we're gonna do. I want each of you to select a car or truck that you'd like. It has to be used, and you can only pick one vehicle. Money is no object, 'cause we aren't actually going to buy anything. I'll give you a little time to make your decision, and then each of you will get a turn to show us the car you picked and tell us the reasons you picked it. Does that make sense?

So far, so good. As they look around the lot, hang with the kids and note what they say, what they look at, etc. You may be able to tie it in later. (Besides, the salespeople may get nervous if they don't appear to have any adult supervision!)

It is very important *not* to volunteer any advice at this point. You're the silent observer. If they ask your opinion, give it. If they comment that a particular car is really cool and they look to see if you agree, hey, be honest. If the car is cool, the car is cool. The fact is, there are probably plenty of cars in the lot *you'd* love to have, right?

Don't drag this on too long. You may have to put a time limit on them to make their picks. Once they've made their decisions, let each of the kids bring you and the others to the car of his choice and tell you what he likes about it.

If you're hearing things like, "I love the look of this," "This one has a great CD player," "This car is so cool," "I love this color," etc., etc., you're right on track. You have them right where you want them to really drive home the point. After everybody has presented his "dream car" or truck, take it to the next level by saying something like this:

You know, most of you said great things about the car you picked. I heard about fun features, favorite models, how clean the car was and good-looking colors. You've probably already imagined how jealous your friends would be if they saw you with that car. Maybe you liked how fast the car was or how expensive it was.

Guys, this is like life. We make some pretty big decisions based on our emotions, based on what we like or what makes us feel good. That happens to a lot of kids when they want

Caution: Age-Level Warning!

Maybe your kids are too young for this topic; if so, pass it by for now. Don't bury it, though. It's too important! Besides, it doesn't hurt to talk about this early, before they start picking up the wrong message from the world around them.

to start dating, and even when they choose the person they'll marry. They base their decision on a person's outward appearance. Just like a car with some nice curves to it, they want to choose a girl or a guy the same way.

Let me share a couple of verses with you.

> Charm is deceptive, and beauty is fleeting; but a woman who fears the LORD is to be praised. (Proverbs 31:30)

> The LORD does not look at the things man looks at. Man looks at the outward appearance, but the LORD looks at the heart. (1 Samuel 16:7)

Tie It Together

When it came to picking the car, I didn't see a whole lot of concern about how the vehicle was *mechanically*. Nobody said, "Gee, this car really looks good to me, but I'd really like a mechanic to go over it before I make a decision." Nobody even attempted to look under the hood. (*If you've got a budding mechanic on your hands, you may have to reword this, but most kids will not have given the engine a single thought.*) Why not?

Input time. A silly question maybe, but try to draw the answer out of them. Maybe they didn't think about it because they assumed the car would run well. Maybe they knew it came with a warranty, or something along those lines. That's fine. Reel 'em in now.

The most important consideration—how the car is mechanically—is often the last thing we think of, if at all. The world has a way of encouraging us to look only at the outside, just like they do in this lot.

It's the same way with dating. Often we let ourselves get "sold" on a person before we understand what's in his heart. Just exactly where is that person spiritually? How real is his relationship with God? Does his life show uncompromising commitment to Christ? Does he possess the unwavering desire to live for Christ? Those are some of the things you'll need in a mate in order to have a great relationship that lasts a lifetime.

If you make a bad decision about a car, you can always trade it for a new one. It doesn't work that way when you get married. Marriage was intended to be for keeps. If you're smart, you'll only want to date a person who is spiritually on track. Sure, personality and looks do their part in attracting too, but a wise Christian won't consider dating someone who is lacking in the spiritual commitment department.

It works the other way around too. What do you think that means for you?

We're looking for your kids to realize that they have to work on their personal relationships with Christ if they want to attract committed Christians. I wouldn't expect them to get that just yet, and even if they do, they may not verbalize it. If that's the case, you need to spell it out for them so they can think about it a bit.

If I want to attract a spiritually on-the-ball person, I'd better be sure I'm really working on my own spiritual life. Otherwise, the person I'd like to date won't even consider me.

OK, they got it. Wrap it up and get out of there before a salesman offers to let you test drive the car you had *your* eyes on.

Guys, beauty really can be a beast. We can get distracted by desirable outward features. We need to remember to let the "Mechanic" (*point your index finger up toward God*) speak to us about the hearts of people we are interested in.

We need to avoid a person whose heart is not all-out dedicated to the Lord or we'll be heading for disaster.

One last thought: Maybe you need to ask the "Mechanic" to give *you* a little tune-up too!

No Foolin'

What's the Point?

You may fool others, but you'll never fool God about hidden sin in your life—and we can prove it!

Things You'll Need

- A roll of quarters
- A 3/4" dowel rod, cut into sections about the same length as the roll of quarters, one for each person (by the way, the more people you have for this devotional, the better)

The whole idea is that one person will have the roll of quarters in his pocket, and each of the others will have one of the dowel rod sections. It will be impossible to tell who actually has the quarters just by looking at them.

The final step in preparation is to arrange a visit to a place with a metal-detecting security checkpoint. When you and the kids stroll through the metal detector, the one with the quarters will set off the alarm. Bingo! A great lesson on how God sees our sin, no matter how clever we are about covering it up.

You can probably find a metal detector at the local police

Here We Go

Get the kids together and start things rolling by saying something like this:

OK, guys. I've got this roll of quarters and some dowel rods here. Here's the deal: I want each of you to empty your pockets and then take one of these and put it in your pocket. One of you will have the roll of quarters; the rest of you will have a dowel rod.

At this point you may run into a small rush to grab for the quarters. They may think that the person who grabs the roll of quarters actually will get to keep them. Kids, huh?

I'm going to leave the room so I don't see who has the roll of quarters. Your goal is to try to fool me. After you've decided who will have the quarters in his pocket, that person must keep it on him until the end of the game. The roll has to be intact. You can't divide it between yourselves.

Now, here's where it will get interesting. I'll have one hour to determine who has the roll of quarters. I will only have one chance to guess, and if I lose, you can divide the quarters between yourselves. If I win, I get the quarters back. Sound fair to you?

They should have no trouble agreeing to your terms, especially when they hear you only get one guess. Now, your kids may want to add their own terms to the deal. They know you have something up your sleeve, and they'd like to derail you if they can. I doubt they'll figure you're taking them to a metal detecting security checkpoint. Anyway, if the conditions they'd like to add to the deal are reasonable, go ahead and agree to them.

OK, I'm leaving the room. One of you put the quarters in your pocket, the others the dowel rods. Now just to make this fair, I want you to empty your pockets of everything else. Call me when you're done. I'll only give you a couple of minutes.

As you get up to leave the room, don't be surprised if they set up some safeguards to make sure you don't cheat. Perfect—that just shows that they haven't figured out how you're going to do it yet. (By the way, it's important that they empty their pockets—you don't want to lose those quarters just because somebody has some other metal on him, do you? Remember, you only have one guess!)

When they call you back into the room, you might say something like this:

OK, let me make sure you did this right. One of you has the full roll of quarters on you right now, and you're going to keep that on you until my hour is up or I make my one guess, right?

They should all agree. They're waiting to see what you think you can do to guess correctly. You may want to pause and stare at each of their pockets. It'll add to the mystery just a little.

station or courthouse; call ahead and ask them for a demonstration. (With all the concerns about security, I wouldn't try this at an airport!)

All right, grab your shoes. We're taking a little ride.

Of course they'll want to know where they're going. Don't tell them. Let them figure it out as you drive. As you drive you might egg them on a little—"You really think you can fool me?"

When you get to the location for your security checkpoint and park the car, they may get the picture as to exactly how you're going to do it. That's OK. Just smile and lead them to the security checkpoint. Let them go in one by one as you observe. If someone sets off the metal detector alarm, the security personnel will ask him to empty their pockets. Bingo. You caught your culprit. You might say something like this:

I think I'm ready to take my one guess.

Name the one who had the quarters. You might get some howling protests about this not being fair. Just smile and take back your roll of quarters. Time to head back to the car and make an application.

Tie It Together

Now at first, I'll bet you thought you had a pretty good chance of fooling me, right?

They may agree or may still be grumbling at this point.

Let me read you some verses.

There is nothing concealed that will not be disclosed, or hidden that will not be made known. What you have said in the dark will be heard in the daylight, and what you have whispered in the ear in the inner rooms will be proclaimed from the roofs. (Luke 12:2-3)

He who conceals his sins does not prosper, but whoever confesses and renounces them finds mercy. (Proverbs 28:13)

Guys, the truth is, there may be some things you think you can get away with. There are probably lots of things you've already done that I never found out about, and you don't want me to.

Sometimes we start thinking we can cover up wrong things in our life. We can allow a little sin in and hide it so others don't find out.

The thing is, you can fool me—easily. But you can't fool God—ever. You need to remember that whenever you're tempted to do something you'd have to hide from me. I couldn't guess who really had the quarters just by looking at you. I'm not equipped to do that. But when I took you to the metal detector, I couldn't miss.

Just because you get away with something for a while, don't think God doesn't see, or care, or that He won't deal with you about it when He decides the time is right. He's like a metal detector—He never misses. Make sense?

You probably won't get much input here. If someone merely nods his head, you're doing good. There may not be much response, but this had to hit home. At this point, you may want to suggest a time of silent prayer in which they can ask God to reveal to them any hidden sin in their life and to cleanse them from it.

When the time is right, end the prayer and wrap it up. You really aren't going to keep those quarters all to yourself, are you? Maybe you can stop on your way home and pick up some donuts or ice cream for the group. You may even mention that it's a lot better to get rid of hidden sin in their lives rather than to hold on to it.

Paint Balls and Prayer

What's the Point?

Why bother praying if God already knows what He's going to do? That's a tough question—and we'll use paint balls to tackle it.

Things You'll Need

Remember the 4' x 4' piece of plywood you used with the "Peter, Paul and Paint Balls" devotional? You'll be using it again, along with the paint ball gun. (You were hoping you'd get to use it again, right?) At the end of that other devotional, the plywood was painted over with the same color as the paint balls to illustrate how love covers a multitude of sins; you'll be using that same side, with paint balls in a matching color. (If you haven't done that one yet, either do that devotional first or paint one side of the plywood before your devoes with a color as close as possible to the paint balls.)

If you'd rather not have the kids fire a paint ball gun, try the alternative with the paint balls themselves, as described in the "Peter, Paul and Paint Balls" devotional.

Here We Go

When you read the topic of this devotional—why should we pray when God knows what He's going to do anyway—you may have thought, "What are you, nuts or something? Maybe we shouldn't even put such a question in our kids' minds!" The truth is, you've probably wondered more than once about it yourself. The kids will question it someday too, if they haven't already. So what do you say we tackle this one together?

Set up the plywood target, grab the paint ball gun and call the troops together. When they see the paint ball gun, you should have no trouble getting them to join you.

Let the kids fire away at the plywood. Shoot at the *unpainted* side of the plywood first. The paint balls should show up great. After a bit, switch the target around so you're shooting at the side painted the same color as the paint balls. This side isn't as enjoyable, is it? You can't see as much of the paint-splattering effect. To get this point across, prompt them with a question something like this:

Is it my imagination, or is the paint ball shooting not quite as fun on this side as it was on the other side of the plywood?

Hey, they may still be enjoying the shooting so much that they didn't notice. Ask them another question:

Which side is more fun to shoot at?

We're looking for them to say that shooting the unpainted side was more fun. They may not say it, but they're probably thinking it. That's OK. Take charge of the paint ball gun and move on.

When you can't see the effects of your shooting, after a while you'd probably lose interest. I mean, what's the point, right? The same thing can happen when it comes to prayer. We shoot up some prayers, but we don't really see anything change. We may think that God already knows what He's going to do, so why bother praying? What difference does it make anyway? Have you ever had thoughts like that?

You can almost be sure they *have* had thoughts like that before. How about you? If so, admit it. It may free them up to talk about it more.

Yeah, I've wondered about that sometimes too. Let me share some verses with you that really emphasize the need for prayer.

> And pray in the Spirit on all occasions with all kinds of prayers and requests. (Ephesians 6:18)

> Be joyful always; pray continually; give thanks in all circumstances, for this is God's will for you in Christ Jesus. (1 Thessalonians 5:16-18)

You do not have, because you do not ask God. When you ask, you do not receive, because you ask with wrong motives, that you may spend what you get on your pleasures. (James 4:2-3)

Tie It Together

You know, I may not understand everything about electricity, but it doesn't mean I give up on it. I use all kinds of electric things, from lights to the TV. I don't actually *see* the electric current, but I know it's there. I know if I touch a bare wire, I can get a shock.

It's sort of the same with prayer: I don't *see* God; I don't always *see* the effects of my prayers, but I know God hears. I can't give up on prayer just because there are parts of it I don't completely understand.

The Bible makes the importance of prayer so clear. Even Jesus spent a lot of time praying.

OK, so we know prayer is important. It's hard to understand *why* it's so important though, right? I mean, doesn't God already have things planned out? Why do we bother to pray?

OK, you've dropped some million-dollar questions on them. Let's see if we get a reaction. Use whatever they give you and add to it as needed.

Sure, God has plans, but prayer is important for a number of reasons. Here are a few:

1. *Prayer focuses my attention on God.* When we pray, we're coming to Him and asking for help or wisdom instead of relying solely on ourselves. That's a good thing. It really keeps things in perspective.

2. *Prayer focuses my request.* What am I asking for? Why am I asking for it? Is this what God would want? If I don't pray, chances are I'm not fully thinking through the things I want. I'm not considering God's perspective.

3. *Prayer tests my faith.* It takes faith to pray. It's good for me to bring things to God and see how He works things out. It will strengthen me, and that's a very good thing. He says prayer is the right thing to do regardless of how I feel. Do I believe Him? Do I trust Him? Then I should pray.

4. *Prayer allows God to work in me.* Often He'll show me that my heart isn't right. He changes me. He prepares me for His answer.

We tend to think God will do what He plans, whether or not we pray. That isn't true. If we don't pray, God certainly can't do what He'd like to do *in* us. Is this making sense?

Get feedback here. You may only get a nod. I'd love to see more input, but we can live with a nod. We're going to wrap things up quick so we don't get them bored.

If we don't pray, God can't do some things *in* us like teach us to focus on Him, build our faith and prepare our hearts. If we don't pray, God also can't do some things He'd like to do *for* us. Remember that verse we read in James a minute ago? "You do not have, because you do not ask God." That's pretty clear. God wants us to pray, whether or not we always see the immediate effect. We have to trust Him—trust Him that praying is as important for us to do as He says, whether or not we understand it or think our prayers make a difference. Sometimes He wants to give us something, but He's just waiting for us to ask. When we ask, He gives, and our confidence in Him gets stronger.

It isn't as much fun to shoot a paint ball gun when you don't see the immediate effects of the paint balls splattering. Prayer can be like that too. The important thing is that even when we don't see the effects of our prayer, we need to keep praying so God can do things *in* us and *for* us!

Some Things Are Black and White

What's the Point?

Despite what our culture says, God still has some absolutes in this day of compromise and "tolerance." A simple locker key will help you shatter the world's view on this issue.

Things You'll Need

All you really need is a locker key. Find a place that has a whole bunch of lockers lined up. This could be a department store, an airport, train station or any other place that rents lockers for short-term use. Go there ahead of time without the kids so you can set things up. Pick out a locker and take the key.

Now if you really want to do this right, grab some snacks that don't require refrigeration—chips, Twinkies, donuts, candy, whatever— and stock the locker before you lock it up. If you can put the snacks in the locker just before your devotional time, include a plastic bag with ice and soda. (Hey, I'm getting hungry here. Let's get started!)

Here We Go

Get the kids together, pull out the locker key and say something like this:

I have a special key here. Anybody have an idea what it opens?

Let them try to figure out where you're headed with this one. That's fine, because it gets them involved.

OK, so this key opens a locker. The question is, *what* locker? Hop in the car—we're going to find out.

They'll probably ask where you're taking them; keep a little mystery in this by just saying, "You'll see." When you get there, park the car and go to the row of lockers. Gather the kids around and hold up the key.

All right, anyone want to venture a guess as to which locker this key will open?

The key probably has the locker number stamped right on it. This looks like a "no brainer" to the kids. For that very reason they may think there's some kind of "catch" to it.

Who's ready to try the key?

Hand the key to your volunteer, and make him try the key in some of the other lockers before going to the right one. He'll probably protest. Just explain that you're trying to make a point. When the key fits and unlocks the right locker, don't let him take the goodies out yet. Find a good spot near the lockers and bring home your application before hitting the snacks. You might say something like this:

All right, that was pretty easy, right? The key has a number, the locker has the same number, and the key opens the locker. The key won't work in any other locker, and any other key won't work in ours. That's what we might call an "absolute." There's no difference of opinion here. There is one key that fits only one locker—period.

If I stopped anybody in this place and ran that statement about the key fitting only one locker by them, they'd have no problem with it; it's a black-and-white issue. One key, one locker—that's the way it works. If a key worked any number of lockers, why bother locking your stuff up?

Pause to be sure they're tracking with you.

The crazy thing is, people understand there are absolutes with things like rental lockers, but they have a whole different perspective when it comes to other issues. They take a so-called "tolerant" viewpoint on issues like abortion, homosexuality and sex before marriage. They don't want to pin issues like these down to an absolute right and wrong.

Is it always wrong to cheat, to lie, to break a promise? A lot of people might answer that question with, "It really depends on the circumstances," or some equally wishy-washy statement. Ask them if there is only one way to get to heaven. Most people want to allow for lots of roads to get there. God doesn't see those as gray areas. They're black and white to Him.

Let me read you a verse:

Jesus answered, "I am the way and the truth and the life. No one comes to the Father except through me." (John 14:6)

Tie It Together

When you get talking to some pretty sincere, philosophical and well-meaning friends, they can come up with some pretty fuzzy logic when it comes to absolutes. God isn't that way. His Word is perfectly clear on many issues. There's right, and there's wrong. Black and white. It's that simple.

Abortion isn't a "choice." Homosexuality isn't an "alternative lifestyle." Sex before marriage isn't "accepted" by God as part of the society we live in today. These things are simply wrong. As far as God is concerned, these are "absolutes."

You can get wrapped up in convincing arguments by people defending their misguided opinions on these issues, or you can take God's Word on these topics. I gotta tell you, God's way is the way we want you to go. It's an easier proposition: God lays out the boundaries; all we have to do is follow His lead.

When you have no absolute right and wrong, you will breed chaos, confusion and eventually a lot of hurt and regret. Does this make sense to you?

Give them time here to express some thoughts they may have. They may have some doubts, or they may challenge you on this: "What if this . . . ?"or "What if that . . . ?" That's OK—it means they're thinking. It's better that they question you openly than hold it in; it gives you a chance to respond.

If they hit you with all those "what if" scenarios, do your best to answer them. Stick with what God says in His Word rather than just giving your opinion. You may want to have some references ready, like where the Bible condemns homosexuality, just in case they challenge you to show them where the Bible speaks of it. Your pastor can help.

They may bring up biblical examples, such as King David, who pretended to be crazy when he was looking for the Philistine king to give him asylum. Was it OK to lie then? Or they may mention how Abraham told the pagan king that Sarah was his sister instead of his wife because he was afraid they would kill him to get her. The answer to these stories is that the people in the Bible were not perfect. David and Abraham tried to scheme their way out of situations they felt had become life-threatening. They should have just trusted God for protection and stuck with the truth.

You may be having a great discussion about this stuff, but don't let it go on too long and become boring. Pull out the snacks and goodies from the locker and let the kids have their fill. You might wrap it up with something like this:

God rewards those who do things His way. He rewards His obedient ones here on earth and someday in heaven. Don't let people mess you up when it comes to absolutes. Some things really *are* black and white, and the Bible is our guide.

Players Wanted

What's the Point?

Believe it or not, a trip to a video arcade will help the kids understand the importance of using the abilities God gives us.

Things You'll Need

You'll need to find a nearby video arcade. You'll also need a little cash; $20 will go a long way for a family.

Here We Go

When you announce that you're going to the local arcade for family devotions, you shouldn't have any trouble getting the kids in the car. If you haven't been to the place before, scope it out ahead of time.

If the game room you go to uses tokens or "power" cards instead of cash, purchase them as soon as you walk in with the kids. The kids need to see you do this. If you're dropping twenty bucks for games, they ought to be thrilled. The important thing is that they see you actually have a charged-up power card or a pocketful of tokens.

The kids will be anxious to use that card or the tokens you've just picked up. You'll want to slow them down by saying something like this:

Let's walk around the place before we play any games. I want to see what they have here. In fact, as we check this place out, you tell me which games you think would be fun to play.

Now stroll around. The kids will be chafing to play the games, but you're in no hurry. Don't go too slow, however, or you'll get the kids irritated and lose some of the momentum of the lesson. Work your way through the place and end up back at the entrance. Hopefully, the kids have seen plenty of things they'd like to play. When you stop, say something like this:

You know, I'm wondering if this was such a good idea in the first place. I wonder if we should just leave. What do you guys think?

Expect to get some negative reaction at your suggestion. They won't want to leave—in fact, they'll wonder what planet you just arrived from. That's perfect. Now, give them some excuses, some reasons you're a little gun-shy of playing. Here are a few:

I've never played some of those games before.

I'm not good at these kinds of games.

I really don't know how to play these games.

I'm afraid I might not do well at the games. I don't want to lose.

I wonder if I should just try some other time.

You get the idea. Give them a few lines and listen to how they react. You may be able to use their input later. OK, time to give in. Don't overdo it.

Yeah, I guess you're right. Let's do it. Lead the way, guys. Which one should we play first?

Play and have a good time. Let the kids pick the games. Don't forget to let the *kids* play, OK? After playing just a couple of games, you might ask them something like this:

Well, should we stop now, or do you want to keep going?

You can bet they'll want to keep going—perfect. Ask them another question.

Do you think we should use up *all* our tokens/credit today?

I'd guess they'll say yes. Their attitude probably will be, "Hey, you spent the money on the tokens or power card already, we might as well use it all up." If that's pretty close to their attitude, great—you've set things up nicely. Play until the credit is gone. When the power card or tokens are all used up, head home or to a fast-food place for a snack. Then it's time to make some sense of your reluctance to play at first.

Tie It Together

You guys must have thought I was crazy when I suggested we leave the arcade without even playing the games. I mean, here I spent good money on the tokens/power card, and I almost didn't use it. What could I have done with those tokens or that power card outside of the arcade?

They should say you wouldn't be able to use it. Good.

Yeah, you're right. I couldn't buy a gallon of milk with the tokens/power card. It only works at the arcade. Let me read you a parable Jesus told:

Read Matthew 25:1-30, or if you have a child who is a good reader, let him read out loud.

Do you see any similarity between my almost *not* using the tokens/power card and Jesus' parable?

Try to get them to talk now. They need to process this a little. Work with any answer they give you and build on it.

Jesus tells the story about a man who entrusts some treasure to his servants. Two of them used what he gave them and gained more with it. One simply buried it. He didn't use it at all. As a result, he gained nothing except the anger of his master.

When I had those tokens/that power card, it was a little like having the treasure that these men in the story had. If I didn't use it, I would have lost out, and you would have too.

God has given each of us gifts and abilities. He gives each of us opportunities to use them. If we don't use them, we lose them. The guy in the story didn't use what his master gave him and so his master took it away from him. How could that happen to us?

Let them talk. They need to sort this out in their minds a little. After you've gotten their input, sum it up with something like this:

A token/power card is a total waste unless you use it. It's no good anywhere else. In a similar way, God has gifted each one of us. He expects us to use the abilities and opportunities He gives us. He may give us abilities to be

used in small or big ways. It doesn't matter. What counts is what we do with it.

Just like with the games, I could make all kinds of excuses why I shouldn't play—I don't know how, I might lose or look stupid—whatever. People do that in life too. They have a thousand reasons why they don't use what God has given them, but all it amounts to is pure selfishness. God isn't buying those excuses. Use it or lose it. You need to use what God gives you. Develop it. Work at it for *His* glory and the good of God's people. If you don't, He may take it away and give it to someone else.

Sometimes you may not have a clue as to what God has given you. You don't feel particularly "blessed" in some way. What do you think God would say to you about that?

This should be interesting, but don't be surprised if they can't come up with an answer. Let's wrap it up.

In the arcade, I didn't know how to play some of the games until I tried. If you try different things, you might find some areas in which God has gifted you. And don't forget His Word. He has entrusted you with all kinds of treasure there. We need to be in it. We need to ask Him to help us develop into a godly person. We need to share His love with others. God gave you His love, and that is a treasure. Don't bury it—spread it around!

Show God's love to others. It's a way to use what God has given you.

I could go on and on here. Play this by ear. You can't expect them to get it all in one fell swoop. You may want to end it so you don't go too long and start to lose them. If they've heard what you've said up until this point, they've got plenty to think about.

End in prayer, and ask God to help each of the kids not to waste what He's given them, but to use it to spread His love.

Fire Drill

What's the Point?

A fire drill becomes the perfect lead-in to talk about escaping another deadly kind of fire: temptation.

Things You'll Need

I'm guessing you have smoke detectors in the house. If not, get some. If you already have one in place, pick up some new batteries. Also, if you live in a two-story home or building, you may want to pick up a chain ladder for a little fire drill.

You could even do this devotional when you're on a trip. Having a fire drill at a hotel could be fun.

Here We Go

Before you start you'll need to customize this for your situation. Map out plans for the family to escape the house in the event of a fire. If the fire blocked your front door, how would you get out? If you have a second story on the house and the stairway was blocked by fire, how would you get out? (That's where the chain ladder comes in.)

Here's what you're going to do with the kids. You're going to go through these scenarios with them. If you *really* want to get them involved, you'll actually run through at least one drill.

If your fire drill involves going out the window, the kids will love it. But use your head here. A fire drill is a good exercise for fire safety, and it will work perfectly for illustrating our point today, but it can be risky. Use only a ladder that is approved as a fire escape; be sure to have a spotter on the ground; supervise exiting the window; follow the instructions that come with the ladder; and finally, if you have any questions, contact your local fire department for advice. (It's also possible, by the way, to use a ladder with a first-floor window, and just climb down three or four feet to the ground. It's much safer, but it is still good practice and a lot of fun to do.)

If you're at a hotel, you'll have to know the fire escape routes and make a trial run down the stairs. (Using a ladder at a hotel is a no-no. Don't even ask me about the time I tied bed sheets together.)

All right, let's get started. Grab the batteries and anything else you need (such as the escape ladder), and call in the kids. You might start out by saying something like this:

All right guys. We're going to talk a little about fire safety.

If you've seen a recent story in the newspaper about a fire, you may want to bring it up. It would be a logical reason to be addressing fire safety at home.

OK. Tell me what you know about fire safety in the home. What are some things that are important?

They should have a pretty good handle on this. They've probably heard it all a dozen times at school. You want to get them involved, and this is an easy way to start things rolling.

The kids may tell you about the importance of smoke detectors and how you have to be sure they have fresh batteries in them. They may tell you that you should have an escape plan if there is a fire. They may even point out that you should stop, drop and roll in the event your clothes catch on fire.

There are plenty of important tips you can pick up from a call to your local fire department. If you aren't getting good feedback from the kids, you'll have to lead them with questions to draw the information out of them.

All right, so I think we can all agree that smoke detectors are a must. They can give us an early warning that we have a fire, and that will give us a much better chance to get out safely. Now if our batteries are no good, our detectors are useless. I have new batteries. Let's change them before we go any farther.

Change your smoke detector batteries and regroup. If you feel stopping now to change batteries will cause you to lose momentum with the devotional, tell them you'll do it after you're done.

Now, if we have fresh batteries and our detectors are working, we're off to a good start. Next, we need a plan of escape. Let's say you hear the smoke detector, and you see a fire is blocking the front door. What would you do? How would you get out?

You're getting them to think. That's good. They're probably enjoying this. Make up a few more scenarios so they have to think through how to escape.

Depending on the location of the phone, you may instruct them to get a quick call out to 911 on their way out. Better yet, they can bring the cordless phone with them. If the ladder is part of one of your escape scenarios, this is the time to present it to the kids. Ideally, you'll actually want to run through a fire drill with them. Escaping a second-floor window with a ladder is an adventurous drill. That probably means the kids will like it a lot.

After you've run through a practice fire drill, get the kids back together. Now you have everything set up perfectly for what you want to teach them.

A fire drill is extremely important. It's crucial to have a plan worked out in your mind as to how to escape a blaze long before you actually have a fire. When a fire is blocking a stairway, that isn't the time to be wishing you'd bought a chain ladder. There's almost

always a way to escape a fire in the home if you have enough warning and you have an escape plan.

Tie It Together

The same principle works for temptation. This can be a deadly "fire" in a spiritual sense. If we give in to temptation, it can certainly burn and destroy anyone who doesn't escape its danger.

Just like we set up some fire-safety principles to avoid being hurt in a fire, we can set up some principles to protect us from the pain of falling into temptation. We can have some safeguards in place, just like we have smoke detectors in our house to warn us of a fire. Any ideas of what might work as a "spiritual" smoke detector?

Let's see what they say. The Bible certainly can give us guidelines to help us identify when we're flirting with temptation. The Bible gives us clear boundaries and warns us not to cross them. There are warnings about doing wrong, about compromising, lust and premarital sex and a ton of other temptations that can hurt our kids.

Being open and honest about things with parents is another. I remember telling my folks about some suggestive things a girl said shortly after I began dating her. It was like a smoke detector going off. They saw danger and helped me distance myself from that relationship.

If the kids need help understanding how we can have "spiritual" smoke detectors as early warnings, you may have to give them a couple of personal examples like the one I've mentioned to get them thinking.

Let me read you a couple of verses.

> . . . but each one is tempted when, by his own evil desire, he is dragged away and enticed. Then, after desire has conceived, it gives birth to sin; and sin, when it is full-grown, gives birth to death. (James 1:14-15)

These verses tell us that generally *we're* to blame when temptation comes our way. Generally it starts in our minds. We think about the sin. We toy with it. That's just as dangerous as playing with matches. We have to guard our minds when it comes to things that may tempt us.

What are some things that you think are big temptations to kids your age?

Listen closely. If they open up a little, be careful what you say. They may be telling you what *they* struggle with too. They may want to see your reaction. If you act like kids who are tempted in that way are stupid or idiots, don't expect your kids to be opening up to you anytime soon.

Here are another couple of verses:

> Hold on to instruction, do not let it go; guard it well, for it is your life. Do not set

foot on the path of the wicked or walk in the way of evil men. (Proverbs 4:13-14)

Hey, if there was a fire blocking the front door, you'd take another route. The same goes for temptation. You need to avoid the flames of temptation. Stay clear of people, places or things that will bring you closer to temptation.

Here's one more verse:

No temptation has seized you except what is common to man. And God is faithful; he will not let you be tempted beyond what you can bear. But when you are tempted, he will also provide a way out so that you can stand up under it. (1 Corinthians 10:13)

Hey, if the door is blocked, there's always a window. God always provides a way of escape when it comes to temptation. We have to be looking for it and be ready to dive through it without hesitation.

One more thing—the phone. Grabbing the phone and dialing 911 is a good idea on the way out of a burning home. We can do the same thing spiritually. What am I talking about?

It's tempting to do too much talking at this point. It gets too preachy and they may tune out if we don't limit ourselves. There are so many great analogies here, it gets hard to stop. We have to though—and fast.

Yeah, we can send out a "911" to God and ask for His help. But do it on your way out! God will provide a way. All right, can anyone sum this up for us?

Nothing tricky or exhaustive here. You're just trying to get them to do a little talking. Hopefully they'll cover the basics. Temptation can be as deadly as a home fire. We need to set up our "smoke detectors" as sort of an early warning system. We need to know the Word so we can recognize the dangers of temptation. We need to avoid temptation and get away from it pronto.

Indiana Jones, 57 A.D.

What's the Point?

"Christianity is boring!" Do your kids ever hear that from their friends? Here's a chance to show them that it's what's inside that counts.

Things You'll Need

$20. Yep, ideally you'll need about $20 for this devotional. Now, if that's out of the question, you can improvise. The whole idea is to take the kids out for a fun time. For me, it was out to a video arcade and then a fast-food joint for some snacks afterward. It cost me about $20.

If you can come up with a different "fun" time that isn't quite as pricey, great. Pick something you know your kids will enjoy. Maybe you'll go miniature golfing or get tickets to a ball game. You might just go exploring on a hike somewhere. Whatever you do, make it as much of a spontaneous adventure as you can. If you're not sure about what to do, ask someone. Your spouse or other parents you know can be great resources.

You may even want to arrange to have one or more of your kids' friends involved.

Here We Go

Grab the bag that has your plans and cash for the evening stuffed inside. Get the kids together, and say something like this:

OK, guys, I've got something pretty exciting here. Check this out.

Pull out the plain paper bag and hold it up. Act like you'd expect them to be excited just by seeing the bag. Now, the kids aren't going to be too thrilled when they see the bag. If they're like my kids, you might get some real wise-guy remarks from them. "Wow, Dad—that *really* looks exciting!" Hey, that's perfect. You have a good start. Say something like this:

OK, the *outside* of the bag may look pretty boring, but what I have inside is pretty good.

Open the bag and tell them about the plans for your night. If your kids are in their teen years, they still may not react with much enthusiasm no matter how much they like the idea. Don't let that throw you. Roll with it and do your best to make it fun.

On the way home, you might stop at a fast-food place to pick up a snack. Try to pick a table that's a little out of the way so you can talk to the kids without too many distractions. You might say something like this:

When I held up that bag with our plans for the night, it didn't look very exciting, right? You probably thought that whatever was *in* the bag was as boring as the bag looked on the outside.

People make that mistake all the time. They make a wrong assumption about something based solely on the way it looks on the outside. It's like the old saying, "Don't judge a book by its cover." Well, today I want to talk a little about one of those areas people tend to misjudge. It's Christianity. People think being a Christian must be one of the most boring things you could do in life. A lot of *Christians* believe that too! Do you agree with me on that point? Do you feel that a lot of people think Christianity is boring?

We're trying to keep them involved here. If they think about it, I'm sure they'll go along with you on your observation. Try to press it further. Ask them something like this:

OK, *why* do you think some people feel Christianity is boring?

See what they say. It may be an eye-opener. They may be giving you a clue as to how *they* view Christianity. They may even describe how they perceive *your* Christian walk. Ouch, that's a tough one, but you wouldn't be alone. Plenty of kids feel their parents' spiritual life is boring. Let's face it, it wouldn't exactly be what you want to hear, but you're better off knowing what they think so you can make some changes. If they see your Christianity as boring, they probably don't have any intention of following in your footsteps. So listen closely—it may turn out to be a good wake-up call.

If that's the case, ask God to help you be more engaged in the Christian battle and able to convey that sense of adventure in daily life to the kids. Anyway, let's keep going.

That's exactly what I did. You want the event to be an adventure, something your kids will enjoy. If it means bringing their friends, do it.

Now, when you decide on what you're going to do, write it down and put it in a plain brown paper bag along with any money you'll need to do it. A lunch-bag size is nice, but anything will work.

Well, the fact is, a lot of Christians probably *do* seem boring, and people naturally assume Christianity is the same way. Christianity isn't supposed to be that way at all. It's an adventure—a battle. A life-and-death contest between two forces. If it *isn't* exciting, it's only because I'm not as engaged in the battle as I should be.

The Indiana Jones movie series depicted a life of adventure that *anyone* would find exciting. Indy struggled against incredible odds in each of his quests. He battled the elements, the Nazis and the forces of evil. He went from one narrow escape to the next.

There was a man who lived in New Testament days who could pass for Indy's ancient predecessor. He was like the Indiana Jones of 57 A.D. Listen to some of the things he did.

> . . . in prison more frequently, been flogged more severely, and been exposed to death again and again. Five times I received from the Jews the forty lashes minus one. Three times I was beaten with rods, once I was stoned, three times I was shipwrecked, I spent a night and a day in the open sea, I have been constantly on the move. I have been in danger from rivers, in danger from bandits, in danger from my own countrymen, in danger from Gentiles; in danger in the city, in danger in the country, in danger at sea; and in danger from false brothers. I have labored and toiled

and have often gone without sleep; I have known hunger and thirst and have often gone without food; I have been cold and naked. . . .Who is weak, and I do not feel weak? Who is led into sin, and I do not inwardly burn? . . .

In Damascus the governor under King Aretas had the city of the Damascenes guarded in order to arrest me. But I was lowered in a basket from a window in the wall and slipped through his hands. (2 Corinthians 11:23-27, 29, 32-33)

Wow—talk about a life of adventure! This guy makes Indiana Jones look like a slacker. Is the Christian life supposed to be boring? Hardly.

This passage describes some of the adventures of Paul. As I was reading some of the things that happened to him, what really stood out in your mind?

OK, we're just trying to get them to open up here and keep you from speaking too much at one time. Hopefully they'll zero in on something—the shipwrecks, the beatings, maybe the escape through the window in the wall. Let's move on.

Paul was a man who really wanted God to use him. A lot of people today *say* that's what they want, but they aren't being honest with themselves. They really want to have fun, or get things, or go after the things they're really interested in. They're not totally giving themselves to God, and as a result, they aren't living the kind of life God would like for them.

Life is a spiritual war. It's made up of a series of battles, most of which we aren't even aware of. Any idea what I'm talking about here?

This is tough, so don't sweat it if they look at you with blank stares. Just keep going. If they do give some input, help them sum it up.

There is this gigantic war going on between God and the devil and his demons. They're fighting over you and your friends and over the soul of every person on earth. The demons want to distract you, to keep you from having personal devotions today. If they succeed, they win a battle and you weren't even aware a fight was going on.

Our whole day goes on like this. Whether we're aware of it or not, God wants to strengthen you to do his work, to be a warrior for him, like Paul was. The devil seeks to weaken you, to get you to put your effort, time and mind on other things.

If you want adventure, if you don't want a boring Christian life, what do you think you should do?

Crunch time here. Let's see if they have the concept. Give them a minute. If they're struggling, ask them something like this:

Let me put it this way. If you think your Christian life is pretty boring, what does that say about the condition of your relationship with Jesus?

Now they're putting it together, even if they aren't verbalizing it. Time to wrap this one up, partner.

Tie It Together

If the Christian life seems boring, it's probably because I'm not giving myself over to Jesus. It probably means I'm not aware of the spiritual battle going on over the simple decisions and things I do throughout my day.

If you want to live an adventurous life, give yourself completely over to God. Don't cut your devotions or prayer time short. We want to be players, not just spectators. If we went to a basketball or football game, had a good time and our team won, we'd be happy, right?

Sure. But the happiness we feel is nothing compared to the heart-thumping exhilaration the athletes on the team feel. Why? They were engaged in the battle. They have pain, exhaustion and disappointment during the game, to be sure, but when the game is over, nothing can match the feeling of victory that they share. They weren't just *watching* the game. They were *in* it.

That's what I want for you. I don't want you to be a spectator. I want you to know the joy of being in the battle, like Paul. In the end, you'll never regret it.

Good Goalie

What's the Point?

A hockey or soccer game will illustrate the importance of keeping seemingly little sins out of our lives.

Things You'll Need

You'll need a little street hockey equipment, like a couple of sticks and puck or tennis ball. Better yet, take the kids to a real hockey game. You could go to a local park district game or buy some cheap seats at a pro game. Now, if hockey is out-of-season when you're doing this, save it for another time or switch to a soccer game. If you go to a soccer game instead, just adapt the text where needed.

Here We Go

I took my kids to a hockey game for this one, so I'll be coaching you from that perspective. Anyway, imagine how the kids will react when you tell them that the biggest part of devotions will be going to a hockey game. They ought to be excited.

Go to the game and have a good time. You don't have to mention a word about the topic for devotions until after the game is over. On the way home, you might say something like this:

OK, guys, what's the whole object of a hockey game?

We're accepting any answer here. They may not be sure where you're going yet. If they say anything about getting goals, you're on the right track. If they're lost as to what you're asking, rephrase the question. "We have two teams out on the ice, each wanting to go home winners. How do the refs determine who wins?"

The team that makes the most goals wins, so the object of the game is to score at least one more goal than the other team does, right?

They should agree, so just keep moving.

The goalie is a key player in this. Tell me about what you observed about the goalies—the gear they wore, how focused they were, whatever comes to mind.

Let them think a little. They may have noticed that he wore more protective gear than other players. They probably noticed that the goalies were very focused, keeping a watchful eye out

162

for an approaching puck. If the kids are making any observations remotely like I've described, congratulations. You have them right where you want them.

The goalie wears more protective gear because he knows guys are going to be taking slap shots at him. He has a bigger stick to help deflect the puck. He stays totally focused so that he doesn't let the puck get into his net.

You know, in life we're supposed to be sort of like a goalie. Let me read you a few verses:

> How can a young man keep his way pure? By living according to your word. I seek you with all my heart; do not let me stray from your commands. I have hidden your word in my heart that I might not sin against you. (Psalm 119:9-11)

> Be on your guard; stand firm in the faith; be men of courage; be strong. Do everything in love. (1 Corinthians 16:13-14)

> Finally, be strong in the Lord and in his mighty power. Put on the full armor of God so that you can take your stand against the devil's schemes. (Ephesians 6:10-11)

What do you think I'm driving at?

Let's see what they say. They may be pretty close or right on the money. Time to start wrapping this up.

Tie It Together

God wants to get us to take this sin thing, even little sins, very seriously. He wants us to be very aware of sin that the devil may try to "slap shot" into our lives.

Can you imagine a goalie who felt it was OK to let a few goals just slide by? No good goalie would do that. He doesn't want the puck to go into the net even once. That goal may be the one that determines the game.

It should be the same with us. God wants us to carefully guard against any sin that would slip into our lives. Just like goals in a hockey game, those sins add up and can defeat us.

So, how can we guard ourselves from little sins that come our way?

Let's see what they say. Take whatever they give you and add to it so they get the picture.

First of all, I guess you have to recognize sin. Watch out for it. Don't let yourself be in a position were you're more vulnerable. What do I mean by that? Think about the hockey game. The goalie is pretty careful not to skate too far away from his net, right? In the same way, we don't want to go places we shouldn't either. We have to be careful we don't put ourselves in a position where it would be harder to resist sin.

That may mean we say "no" to some activities or friendships. We have to be careful what we watch, what we listen to. We have to watch the attitude we have. The devil can use any one of these, and plenty of others, to try and slide sin in your life. He wants to defeat us. Does this make sense?

You have to ask this question. You need to see if they understand. You can end it right now if you think they've gotten the message. If you go too long, you'll lose their interest anyway. You don't want the kids to feel like they just got put in the penalty box. If you sense they want to talk more, great. Let them talk, then draw it to a conclusion.

A good goalie uses his protective gear and all the skill he has to keep the puck from entering his goal. We want to be a good goalie with our life. We want to use the protection that God provides for us in His Word and discipline ourselves to keep sin out of our lives.

Other Books
by Tim Shoemaker

Tried and True Job

Wearing the Mask

Smashed Tomatoes, Bottle Rockets
. . . and Other Outdoor Devotionals You Can Do With Your Kids